PRINCIPAL TO PRINCIPAL

Conversations in Servant Leadership and School Transformation

Rocky Wallace

Rowman & Littlefield Education
Lanham, Maryland • Toronto • Plymouth, UK
2008

Published in the United States of America
by Rowman & Littlefield Education
A Division of Rowman & Littlefield Publishers, Inc.
A wholly owned subsidiary of The Rowman & Littlefield Publishing Group, Inc.
4501 Forbes Boulevard, Suite 200, Lanham, Maryland 20706
www.rowmaneducation.com

Estover Road
Plymouth PL6 7PY
United Kingdom

British Library Cataloguing in Publication Information Available

Library of Congress Cataloging-in-Publication Data
Wallace, Rocky, 1956–
Principal to principal : conversations in servant leadership and school transformation / Rocky Wallace.
p. cm.
Includes bibliographical references.
ISBN-13: 978-1-57886-759-2 (hardcover : alk. paper)
ISBN-10: 1-57886-759-2 (hardcover : alk. paper)
ISBN-13: 978-1-57886-760-8 (pbk. : alk. paper)
ISBN-10: 1-57886-760-6 (pbk. : alk. paper)
1. School principals–United States. 2. Educational leadership–United States. 3. School management and organization–United States. I. Title.
LB2831.92.W346 2008
371.2'012–dc22 2007040833

Manufactured in the United States of America.

This book is dedicated to my wife, Denise, and our two teenage daughters, Lauren and Bethany. They stood by me every step of the way as they realized I needed to plunge into the demands of doctoral study. Ladies, thanks for letting Dad use the computer whenever I needed to. And Denise, thanks for helping me with my research. To the three of you: I love you all so very much and am blessed beyond measure to get to travel through life with you by my side.

CONTENTS

PREFACE

In today's world of rapid change, where the stakes are high and many struggle to find their purpose, the role of the school principal is one of the most important leadership positions in our society. Here, we take a walk through the course of one school year, as seen through the eyes of a retiring principal and his successor. As the veteran gently and carefully coaches and listens to his young student, what unfolds is the transformation that every school is capable of—when led by a servant leader who is willing to abandon self, tradition, and status quo in order to push every member of the school community to heights previously thought unreachable.

Is such a call for the reinvention of the schooling process really necessary? Aren't American schools getting better every year? The reality is, the education system in the United States is in trouble, given the global knowledge economy that is now driving every aspect of the American culture. But there is hope, if educational leaders will lead their schools through the maze of contradictions and focus on core values—core values that are built around relationships, a thirst for excellence, and a commitment to children first—every day, in every way. Doing the right things, at the right times, for the right reasons: it almost sounds too simple!

ACKNOWLEDGMENTS

This book would not be possible without the wise counsel of my Regent University mentors, especially Bruce Winston and Jacque King. The Regent model is a cutting-edge doctoral program that immersed me in the study of servant leadership for the past four years. My life will never be the same.

I will always appreciate the support of Stan Riggs and the Kentucky Educational Development Corporation, and my colleagues at KEDC. To my KEDC family, I simply say thank you. What good and talented people to have the privilege to work with every day as we serve our colleagues down in the trenches in our schools and classrooms!

I will be forever grateful to Morehead State University for the encouragement of my professional colleagues on the university level—Dale Duvall, David Barnett, Dan Branham, Ben Dickens, and Hobart Harmon. Without their friendship and guidance, I might not have made that all-important first step four years ago and embarked upon my doctoral journey.

Finally, I would be remiss if I did not give credit to Bill Capehart, my former superintendent, who encouraged me as a principal seven years ago to chase my dreams. And, likewise, I owe gratitude to Jim Jackson, who helped make those dreams come true when he hired me to work with him at the Kentucky Department of Education in January 2000 as we followed our hearts and offered support to school principals out in the field.

And to all those principals, wherever they might be, who serve our schools, I simply say: You are gentle giants, and heroes and heroines in your communities, as you stand in the gap, leading your flock toward home.

But in the beginning, when I was just a child, it was Mom and Dad who instilled in me the critical importance of going to college as a key passage into the fascinating world of learning and discovery. Mom and Dad have always modeled so well the premise that we must live each day by a sound set of core values. They and my younger siblings—Debbie, Robin, Mark, and Barbie—always believed in me and encouraged me to stay focused on the road less traveled. And that truly has made all the difference.

1

SELF-LEADERSHIP

A servant leader empties self of self, so others may prosper.

John looked around his office, wondering where the years had gone. Earlier that week, he had said good-bye to his staff, his students, and the community. Yesterday, he had boxed up all of his belongings. Now, all that was left was a morning conversation with his successor—a new "kid" just beginning her career as a school principal. John had promised the superintendent he would stick around one more day and do a short orientation. Although drained from a very emotional week, he knew he needed to do this. He wanted this school to keep climbing, and he wanted his team and the students to not lose the magic they had built in recent years.

Remembering his first year as a principal, John wanted to pass the torch with some final mentoring, knowing that once he handed over the keys later that morning his work was finished. Never again would he have this opportunity, so he saw these next three hours as his gift to this life work and the people he so loved. As he heard the knock on his office door, his heart jumped for a second. "Give me strength, Lord," he prayed silently, as he had done so many times here in this office over the years.

"Come in, Linda. Great to see you. Let me shake your hand—congratulations on being named the new principal here at Heritage Elementary. I have heard some great things about you and your success as a teacher."

"Well, John, that's a real compliment coming from you. I must tell you, I am very nervous to be following a legend in this community and trying to somehow fill your shoes."

"Linda, you will do fine and are just what this school needs at this stage of its growth. You love kids, and you are so good with people. With those two graces, the rest of it will fall into place. But before I start rambling on here, let's just sit and let you ask me some questions. I promise not to overwhelm you."

"OK. I guess what has kept me up at night already is worrying about the endless responsibilities that I will be in charge of. I am so new and so green. How did you deal with the feelings of inadequacy your first year or two?"

"Great question. I've already answered it in part. You have such a great reputation, Linda, for loving people and serving others. More than anything else you do and experience this first year, do not ever let yourself drift away from this core value of caring for others. You build organizations that succeed by putting people first. So whatever the type of work, the success is going to boil down to one thing: the relationships among the people that make up the organization."

"But what about curriculum, student discipline, test scores, the many diverse views, keeping the parents on board, keeping the staff together as a team? It just seems so overwhelming!"

"It is overwhelming if you think you have to control all of these variables, but you don't. Instead, by focusing everyone who is involved with this school in any way on what is the most important, all of these parts will come together."

"Is this how you excelled so well as a principal over the years?"

"Well, yes, in my latter years. But I must admit, I struggled miserably in my early years because I was so busy trying to be a principal, I forgot how to be a good person who simplified every day by doing what was best for the kids and then just serving. When I figured it out, I was able to let so many things go. My wife and our kids told me that's when I changed, and my staff told me the same thing."

"So did the problems stop coming to you? Did parents stop complaining? It sounds wonderful to just let it go!"

"No, I still had fires to put out every day. But once I began to self-lead and empty myself of self, they no longer seemed like fires. They were opportunities for me to help others. But I had to get my self-importance and pride out of the way first. There is a dark side to leadership—blind spots of self-deception that can cause hurt to self and others. All leaders have this potential for disaster, but not all leaders can look in the mirror and admit it. In fact, this is a phenomenon that is impacting our American culture in a major way today—a decrease in the cultural understanding of, and need for, moral absolutes."

"But how did you actually make such a bold change in your personality, your management style?"

"Well, I mainly did one thing differently that I hadn't ever taken the time to learn before: I began to truly listen to others. I stopped talking so much, I began to take notes, and I listened. Most of the time, others had the solutions to all those problems I had previously felt like I had to fix every day."

"OK, I think I get it so far. But, John, surely changing self doesn't guarantee that others will buy in to what you are modeling. The school I just left spent a lot of time on trainings and workshops—but let me tell you, we had major issues, even among staff."

"Exactly. The leader is the catalyst for change, but it sometimes takes years to transform the toxic culture that you are alluding to. This whole concept of serving others, which is originally found in the New Testament by the way, is not just a theory—it's a way of life. My lead professor in grad school paralleled this theory of 'upside down' leadership to Jesus' Sermon on the Mount. It calls on every member of the organization to start thinking about the ethics and values that need to be in place. It transforms political committees to trusting, effective teams. It calls on the community to jump into sacrificial support of the kids and the school. It challenges the school board to resolve its differences and become cheerleaders for what's going on in the classroom. It eventually ingrains in the students the whole concept of a learning community, where cooperation and developing into well-rounded, educated contributors to the larger society is the vision."

"So, servant leadership theory, even if just modeled initially by the principal, impacts the entire system, even board members? Even unhappy and burned-out teachers? Even the most rowdy kids?"

"I will just say this, Linda—Heritage was a broken school when I came here as principal ten years ago. It was still a broken school five years later until I finally admitted that the change was going to have to begin with me. When I let go, as we are phrasing it, that is the day this school, community, and yes, even our relationship with the district office and board began to change."

"John, I am changing from being sick to my stomach with nervousness to an excitement that I can't describe! So, I bet, with this whole leadership system you were molding getting stronger every year, the job just got easier and easier."

"Yes and no. First, it was not about 'me,' but all of us working together and giving each other a whole lot of grace. I even shifted to focusing our professional development and teacher's meetings much more to core values, ethics, the holistic needs of our students, and how to build healthy and trusting relationships with parents and other staff members. We asked ourselves what followers would expect most from us as an instructional team in leading this school. We studied the literature on values-driven leadership. We even changed our morning announcement structure to include much more values-driven content. The kids would rather hear a quote by Abe Lincoln any day of the week than just the usual chatter."

"Did you ever sleep? When did you relax? I can see where transforming an entire organizational system could consume a person."

"Good question. Actually, Linda, I found I had more time to be at home with my family. I was finally empowering others to share their talents and ideas much more than I had previously, and this helped my emotional health more than can be measured. I was able to set aside time for my daily 'quiet time' and devotional reading again, and relax with my hobbies. Plus, with this new freedom, I was able to start watching my sleeping and eating habits more. I also got into a good exercise routine. This attention to personal health is crucial. So many of my colleagues at other schools have had health problems over the years—many of them emotion-related."

"John, you seem so at peace. I envy you. We just did not have this type of culture at my former school, although we certainly tried to improve every year . . . by the way, can we break for a minute? My head is spinning, and I want to learn all I can from you. I'm going down the hall to get a drink of water. Be right back."

In Leading Change, *O'Toole (1996) reveals that leaders routinely resist the very change they have helped champion for the organization.*

SUMMARY

John shares with Linda, in their very first conversation, that before he truly learned how to lead others, he had to start with himself. Once he looked in the mirror and admitted his humanness, he then began to approach life differently. He identified his core values and prioritized, thus taking more time to stay in good physical, mental, emotional, and spiritual shape. And he did not let his job replace his family. They came first. As a result of learning to hold himself accountable, he was then able to model well for his staff, thus gaining their respect as he emphasized principles and balance in his life and in the school's culture, too.

2

STRUCTURE AND PROCESS

An organization is a system, finding harmony through coordination of all its parts.

John looked around the office as he waited for Linda. He flashed back to memory after memory. He smiled as he thought of the many times his kids had come to work with him in the summer months, and what a joy that had been. How proud they had always been of their daddy! Linda soon returned with a bottle of water for John as well.

"OK. Now, where were we, John?"

"Linda, don't feel like you need to beat up on your old school. They do a lot of things very well there. I know your former principal, and I know what a time he had with the structure and process piece."

"Structure? Process?"

"Yes. This is the piece that all organizations spend so much time on and so few get right. And it took us years here to figure out what ours needed to look like. Finally, one summer, in the midst of our annual strategizing that we rarely implemented, someone stood up and said to the whole group: 'What are the essentials we know we need to work on for the coming year?' Well, it was almost too easy after that! We knew by then what our core values were, and we were living them all around the building. We spent the rest of that day coming to agreement on our vision and mission, making sure our core values were aligned as they should be. The next day we developed a large list of priorities and then narrowed them down to three short-term goals for the following year. Then, we plugged in specific strategies for each goal, and who was going to help get them implemented."

"But what happened after the school year started?"

"We committed to hold each other accountable, so we agreed as a faculty to spend group time together each quarter to self-assess our progress on this one-year plan. We have never stopped with this simple process. Every three months, we review and refine our plan, looking at student data, surveying parents, and then wrapping customized professional development around our most urgent needs. To keep us focused and at the cutting edge of our field, we do staff book studies all the time. During that first summer, I remember we read a book that focused on strategic thinking in the midst of chaos. This whole process is a wonderful, practical model that we all believe in, and it has changed how we run our school. Now, everyone knows exactly what our goals and strategies are and how we're going to implement them."

"But what about the master schedule? Teacher assignments? What classes are offered? At my old school, we argued on this every spring and half the summer!"

"All of this falls into place when the staff together assesses student needs, then agrees upon vision, mission, core values, goals, and strategies. Then, we all just work this model—over and over. Even the kids know the school's vision, mission statement, and core values. We don't just write it all down somewhere. We live it."

"Wow. And it's not chaotic, with all the staff positioning for their own agendas, their own rooms, their own student rosters?"

"No, not anymore. Oh, make no mistake, there is always a positive turbulence, a healthy tension if you will, as we never stop looking for more effective ways to serve our students and prepare them for a future of endless possibilities. Such a culture never rests on its laurels because every year brings new kids, new challenges, new technology, new partners who want to help us. But remember, we have spent years focusing our professional development on servant leadership, values, ethics—and how all of this relates every day to how we treat our kids, each other, and our many other partners. So we have become what I would call an 'authentic' learning community. By that I mean that we relentlessly hold each other accountable."

"You keep saying you hold each other accountable. What does that look like?"

"My teachers learned to feel free to come in and tell me when I had handled a situation poorly or overlooked something. I, in turn, then had the true freedom to sit down and talk to them in a vulnerable and real way about growth areas they needed to keep working on. And in terms of resolving internal conflict, we all learned to take the time to schedule the meetings and talk out the issues—with parents or anyone in our total school community. We only had three rules: 1. Be honest. 2. Be gentle, with lots of grace. 3. And listen—so we truly understand the other's perspectives."

"So, John, really, you were able to go beneath the surface as an organization and address ethical or gray-area issues that most people just leave alone, hoping the right thing will be done eventually?"

"Exactly. How can human beings always do the right thing if they are not held accountable? There absolutely must be well-defined boundaries and also a support system in place. The first thing I did when a new teacher was hired for our school was to match him or her with a mentor who would be there for support in any situation. And all of our staff were required to have an active one-to-one coaching/mentoring partnership in place. Sometimes, this accountability partner would actually teach in another school."

"Like you are doing with me this morning?"

"Right. How can we do the right things, at the right times, for the right reasons if we're not even talking regularly about the various situations we find ourselves in? At Heritage, we realized we could not build this type of culture if we had even one 'lone ranger.' I had an accountability partner and mentor too. The first book he had me read was about leading change. It really opened my eyes to how critical the leader is in blessing others so that change can really happen. Often, the leader is the one who deep down really doesn't want change to take place."

"Did any staff ever quit over this high level of expectation and accountability?"

"A few, but not many. In recent years, our entire school district has devoted much attention to organizational structure and creating a holistic system with a unified and healthy culture. We believe in the 360 leader model. In essence, this philosophy sees every person, on all levels, as a leader—impacting others in various ways every day. So we don't develop school-level teams with just our parents and community leaders involved."

"What do you mean? Who else would be involved in helping with your school?"

"We also have an array of district-level teams, which really helps all of us to connect the dots. Technology is a great example. Just a few years ago we were, in many ways, a series of isolated schools answering to the same central office and school board. Now, what goes on here at Heritage very much impacts what goes on throughout the district. Our hiring policies, evaluation system, increase in extracurricular opportunities for students, use of facilities after school and in the summer, even the vision and core values of the school board—we all are interconnected. This certainly holds you accountable as the leader of the school, Linda. But it also gives you a network of support that you will learn to tap into every day."

"So the entire school district and all its schools are in agreement that we all should be working as one?"

"Yes, this new culture of a shared, integrated learning community is a work in progress, but we're getting there. We are a loosely coupled system, with each school having autonomy and freedom to make decisions that are in the best interest of its students and community. But we are also an organization that operates very similarly to a spider plant. We have the one central core of the plant—our board and district office. Then we have each school community shooting off that core. And when we share ideas and resources, the synergy is powerful."

"Oh, I don't know if I like that. Looks like my school could easily be swallowed up in the agendas of the larger schools or those that the school board favors."

"Well, in the old days, that was very common. But, Linda, remember, we're transforming into a system that is driven by core values and a spirit of team and community. We are now both an organism and an organization. The old political games are snuffed out when individuals and school communities start focusing on relationships and the good of all the kids—not just those in a particular zone of the county. It's the mathematical reality that one plus one does not always equal two. With synergy, magic can result."

"So if I go to a school board meeting later this fall and ask for something that is not in my budget but that we need for our students, there's a chance they will consider it?"

"In the old days, the answer would be based on who you know, what board member represented your school, and if you and your staff were considered politically savvy or not. Today, if you do indeed take a request to the board that is not already in the annual strategic plan and budget, they will listen, they will ask for thorough research, and they will automatically look for ways that your idea could possibly also be used to help other schools. Now that's an organizational system that is smart and learning to exist in the twenty-first century."

"I recently read that the main reason Wal-Mart was able to overtake Sears and other retail giants was because of the traditional front-runners being so sure of their policies and practices that they couldn't change their paradigms to adjust quickly enough to Wal-Mart's new model."

"Linda! You're getting it! Yes! Wal-Mart's 24/7 customer service was so radical, no one would dare believe it would work. What if we in the school business operated more like Wal-Mart—just out there, doing what our customers need—regardless. Well, that's what our district, as a unified whole, is focused on. And it's making a huge difference."

"What about other schools in the region or around the state? I always wanted to devote part of my annual professional development plan to visiting successful models away from home, but never got a chance to do that."

"Our superintendent has been equipping the principal team with more and more global leadership opportunities. He preaches that our school district must learn to be a boundaryless organization, and has required the principals to explore the research on how to look for better answers in preparing for a future that is changing at a record pace. He says that when we are riding a wave of success, then that momentum will carry us on to the crest of the next wave. So, when succeeding, that's when you take more risks! This theory, by the way, has major implications for traditional schooling and the old guard that does not want to see much changed. But yes, you and your staff will have resources available to visit cutting-edge schools and to bring back successful teaching and learning practices that can keep taking this school and the district to a higher level. If I were you, I'd also start taking parents with me to regional and state education conferences and meetings."

"Good idea. I have just never heard of that being done much."

"We wonder why more parents aren't supportive of our schools, but really, do we include them in the information and decision-making circle as we should? No, up to this point, we have not. But now, with the Internet opening up access to information from all over the world, this new global economy is spreading the knowledge capital around as never before. Just this summer, a team of five educators from our district is visiting Europe, and two of our board members are spending a week in China. It's all interconnected, as never before. Schools that don't grasp this reality will struggle to the point of possibly becoming extinct in the near future. Parents will have little interest in sending their kids to the local community school if it is out of touch with state-of-the-art instruction and learning that is going on all around it in neighboring schools."

John stopped for a short break, as Linda needed to go out to her car to grab another notepad. She had been trying to write down everything John said all morning. Again, his memory flashed back to his first day in this office. That evening, his wife had baked a cake to celebrate and had invited family over. It seemed just like yesterday.

In The Fifth Discipline, *Senge (1994) cautions that learning organizations must resist the temptation to continue to exist on yesterday's solutions.*

SUMMARY

As John stresses the importance of process, Linda realizes that leading a school is not just about the day-to-day routine and schedules. Much more important are the structure and strategies—how a system is designed so that it utilizes all the available resources to reach its goals. She also learns that a school will not reach maximum effectiveness if not aligned with a common purpose with the school district it belongs to. The interconnectedness and relationships with stakeholders and partners will make all the difference in how her school becomes a welcoming, serving, child-centered, learning community.

3

VISION

Without a compass, the ship tossed to and fro throughout the night.

"John, you have mentioned vision a couple of times. I've never really heard it explained as the driving force of a school. Tell me more."

"Well, I hadn't either, earlier in my career. But one day, a dad came in and challenged me to share with him our school's purpose for existence. He had played ball for a very successful coach in college and had been groomed to set high goals, and then do whatever it took to achieve them. He said he never saw anything about our school's vision in notes he received from his child's teacher. Quite frankly, I was stumped. All I could think of to say was that our hope was to prepare every student for optimum fulfillment in life.

"He simply said, 'Then why did the school district drop its elementary band program this past year? Why do the kids only have art about twice a month? Why don't you have a modern science lab in this school? Why aren't there more clubs to meet the diverse interests of your student population? Why aren't the community's civic leaders in these classrooms on a regular basis sharing insights with these kids about going to college and what it will take for them to truly chase their dreams?'

"I had no smooth, 'educator lingo' comeback. And he was not finished. He went on to say, 'You are not living your vision for this school. You are playing by the same old rules in a system that is broken. Next year, my kid is going to a school that has an inspiring vision and then goes after it—every day!'

"Linda, I never again went into planning for a new school year without establishing very specific goals that were focused on what our kids needed—not just on what the school district has always provided. The school board probably got tired of seeing my parents, teachers, and me coming to their meetings, but from that point we definitely were a school with vision. You see, working day to day, by the standard rules, with your head down, can move an educator through a career—but that's not what teachers go into education for. They go into teaching to change lives. So that's what we do around here. If a teacher here doesn't buy into that vision, he or she won't fit into this faculty at all."

"Wow! It must be exciting to work here!"

"There's never a dull moment. We have spent a lot of time the past couple of years extending our vision into the future, asking ourselves what we could be here at Heritage in the future. Your first council meeting will include the unfolding of a preferable future that includes an intramural program that will have every student on at least one sports team, a volunteer program that will have every parent involved in at least one service project for the school, and an outdoor learning center that will actually be a five-acre nature park, complete with vegetable gardens that students will help maintain."

"Oh, how exciting! But John, is this really the role of the twenty-first-century school, to expand its services to such a degree?"

"Let me put it this way. Scanning the environment, looking globally at what other education systems are doing, realizing the independent learning that can now take place at home due to the miracles of technology—the future includes the reality that American schooling is no longer a monopoly. If schools don't meet the needs of the market—to use a business principle—they may not even be relevant in ten to twenty years. This is a scenario that many educators don't want to talk about, but it's taking place right now. Schools without a well-planned and articulated vision—and without a process in place to follow through and implement it—are in real trouble."

"Now you've got me a little scared, John. I thought I was here to manage and organize, to be the gatekeeper."

"Look at it more like the role of shepherd, steering your flock in a direction away from danger and into a bright future with endless possibility. So this is like a creativity piece that you must devote a considerable amount of your time and energy to."

"Creative piece? I thought I was to empty myself of myself and simply serve."

"That's often what our culture teaches, isn't it? Those who serve are meek, passive, and just sort of let the 'movers and shakers' make the big decisions. But the mature leader will automatically be engaged in empowering and equipping all of his or her human resources so all that energy can be integrated into a powerful force for positive change. Your most important days will be the days that you set aside time to be creative and innovative, and share those ideas back and forth with your staff, parents, and other partners. Make sure you get away from being a prisoner to paperwork and day-to-day urgent—but not important—tasks and think outside the box, constantly looking for better answers."

"Better answers? You mean like more effective teaching? A smarter way to do bus routes? What to do with the brightest kids when they are bored half the time? How to truly meet the individual needs of the kids in special education? All that stuff that seems to somehow never change much?"

"Exactly. You and your staff are social scientists and inventors of new ideas, whether you realize it or not. Don't ever let yourselves get caught in a rut, being swallowed up with policy and bureaucracy. Educators are the professionals who have been trained to open up minds to the endless wonders of what could be! But instead, too often, we wallow in a very uninspiring culture of routine—day after day after day. I tell you, in that type of classroom, I don't see how the kids stand it! It would certainly kill my thirst for learning."

"But, John, you know how our district budget formula is designed. Basically, we are funded at twenty to twenty-five students per classroom."

"Then if there is truly no way to change that, it's time to mobilize the volunteers as never before. Perhaps we have looked at it backwards all along. Perhaps the trained teacher should be the facilitator of a learning center that has tutors and other 'helpers' working with kids all day long. There is a better way, Linda, to do 'school,' and those who have figured it out are light years ahead."

In Scenario Planning, *Ringland (1998) challenges the organization to envision a future with endless possibilities and then strategically focus on such scenarios of abundance (thus, not leaving the future to chance and the worst-case scenarios).*

SUMMARY

John throws a new concept at Linda that she had not heard explained in her young career. He teaches her about vision and urges her to dream big for this school, and to help her staff and the school community to dream big, too. He cautions that daily rituals that do not focus on creativity and a future with endless possibilities are dangerous. Linda's job as a servant leader is not just to take care of and protect the school but also involves inspiring the school to embrace needed change.

4

LESSONS LEARNED

In my youth, I painfully learned how to walk the narrow road toward home.

"John, this has been awesome. I had just not thought of my role as the leader of this school as being so inspiring and full of much more than just typical school days, schedules, and solving problems. But before you go, I wanted to make sure I asked you what you would do differently if you could change a few things as you look back over your career. Is that OK?"

"I would be glad to. Oh my, there are lots of things that I would redo if I could. Mainly, I would have become a true servant leader a lot sooner. I regret those early years when my career was all about me and control. . . . I would certainly handle my relationships with my students' parents differently. They only want someone to listen, to let them share their ideas on how the school can be improved. We too often shut them out and make them feel like outsiders. . . . I would spend more time turning kids loose to do creative learning and exploring. Each child is unique, so to treat all of them with these cookie-cutter plans is just ludicrous." John stopped for a second, and gazed out the window with a distant look on his face.

"What else, John?"

"I would have fought harder for more trained staff and volunteers. That makes the biggest difference of all—getting the students the one-on-one and small group help they need—especially in their early years. . . . I would have invested more time, research, and staff into reading and math. Way too many kids are still dropping out of high school or not succeeding in college because they can't read well. Most do not have strong math skills. . . . I would have raised the funds for more science equipment and then required my teachers to use it. Many kids don't like science because they have not been truly exposed to hands-on science. . . . And I would have fought harder for the arts—music, drama, dance, P.E., foreign language, art classes—we really are shorting kids in our American culture by neglecting these disciplines as an integral part of the total curriculum package."

"Thanks, John, for being so honest and real. What would you advise me to stay away from?"

"Oh boy, this can be a long, long list. For sure, stay away from sharing your opinion too much unless you know you really need to say it. People in this culture repeat, and add to, what others have shared so much that no conversation is truly confidential these days. I am convinced of that. It's a very toxic and dangerous element of our society, and the gossiping and 'he said/she said' mentality can just cripple a school community. Also, stay away from beating around the bush too much with personnel issues. If an employee is struggling or has crossed the line, he or she needs help—and fast. Keep ongoing coaching and growth plans going for all staff, and sit down and discuss progress regularly—not just once a year during evaluation season."

John stopped for a moment, looked Linda square in the eye and added, with emphasis in his voice, "Finally, remember, Linda, it's about the people, not just the test scores and data reports. Love those kids, learn their names, and schedule lots of fun and meaningful 'extra' stuff for them as part of the total school experience. Advocate for them first. You may be the only one on that day who's in their corner. And love your staff. They need to be patted on the back for the faithful work they do. They need to be recognized for birthdays and other celebrations. They need you to get to know them, to laugh with them, cry with them, and care when they have experienced a loss. This is what will make you a principal with purpose—not all the other stuff. It must never replace your role in building meaningful, honest, supportive relationships. You've probably heard of emotional intelligence. It's the most important and improvable of all the various intelligences."

"But how do I find the time? It seems like an impossible task to be able to schedule in all this 'people' stuff. I know I should do this, and I want to . . . but how?"

"Personally, each week, I make both a priority list and also a list of things not to do. I have been trying this for several months. Let me tell you—it works. By identifying that which is not the most important, I am then able to do the most important first—and that includes the 'people stuff' before anything else."

"John, I now know why you are considered one of the finest men in this community and why the school district is going to miss you so, so much. I want to tell you something. I will not let you down. I will look at my notes regularly and be there for this school as a servant leader."

"I know you will, Linda. And this staff will help you. They will be undergirding you with a support system that will make this the most unbelievable journey of your life. I have been preparing them for this moment from the first day I arrived as their principal ten years ago. There is not one person on this team here at Heritage who doesn't know the role he or she is to play. They are all in their strength areas, in their niches. They all know how critical the culture is in maintaining a healthy organization. I knew my successor would need to find this place in tip-top shape, ready to roll into another era, soaring higher. In my closing remarks to the staff last week, I reminded them of what you would need—their support, their maturity, their love, their servant leadership. There was not a dry eye in the room."

John stood up and stepped toward the door, then he stopped. "I will be honest with you here. I could not have done this job for ten years without this team believing in me and letting me develop as a caring leader who understood the big picture of the role I was supposed to play."

"John, may I call you from time to time, when the pressure gets great or I just need to ask a question?"

"Oh mercy yes, you know you can. I love this place. A big part of my life was invested here. If you don't do well, then I will not have left this school in the shape you needed to find it in when you arrived. So by all means, call me anytime!"

"Well, where do I begin? I mean, tomorrow, when you are not here, and it's me here in your office?"

Tears welled up in Linda's eyes as she realized John was reaching into his pocket and getting ready to hand her the keys. She was trembling as she wondered, "Can I do this job? He is a legend. I am a rookie! Can I do it?"

John could sense her stress and simply said, "First thing for you to do today is to go home to your family and friends and go out to supper. Celebrate this major 'moment in time' in your life. Then, every day, go home to them with your heart and mind totally on them once you're home. Don't take this work home with you. You won't last ten years if you do that, I can assure you. Also, do what I finally learned to do: put your health above this school."

"And how does one pull that off, John?"

"Set aside specific time for rest and renewal. Eat right, sleep plenty, exercise regularly, and take care of your mental, emotional, and spiritual well-being. That means quiet time and prayer time every day with your Creator, walks in the woods, vacations and retreats, weekends away with your family and friends, enjoying every minute with them, rest on weekends, time for Sabbath, enjoying your hobbies—in other words, the balance of life, the all of life. It goes by so fast. One day, you will be older, your kids will be grown, your husband will be retiring, and you will be handing these keys to someone else. Linda, carpe diem! Every day! Seize the day!"

"Seize the day? Oh, I love it! But, John, how do I sell such a philosophy?"

"Well, it's not always easy, but you need to find a way to convince your staff to buy into it. It is crucial for adults to learn how to shift from success to significance. We have several teachers in our school district who have hit the wall, suffering from burnout. There is a body of work out there now that says the true culprit behind burnout is the organization. So, Linda, whether you want to believe this or not, our school district, this school, me, you—we are part of the problem when staff are experiencing burnout. Admitting this reality will free you to never push staff to do things for the sake of the organization that are unreasonable."

"Oh, to get them all on the same page, John. I just know that when they start coming in to greet me tomorrow, they will have so many unique views and things they need. How do I treat them all with respect for diversity while still molding them into a strong team?"

"A couple of years ago, our staff went through a very thorough professional development on how to build and maintain effective teams. It sure wouldn't hurt to do a refresher course. It would help you, and them, to start seeing this new partnership as 'us.' This makes all the difference."

John handed over the keys, shook Linda's hand, gave her a hug, and he was gone. On his drive home, the tears rolled down his cheeks. What a journey he had been on these past ten years. He loved Heritage and all its people. He would miss them so! But he had served them well—every day. And that had made all the difference. As he pulled up in his driveway, his wife, kids, parents, other relatives, and many, many friends greeted him with a retirement celebration that went on for hours. And guess who also came by? Linda and the entire staff from school. John just cried and laughed all at the same time, as he heard his Father quietly say, "Well done, son. Well done."

In The Human Equation, *Pfeffer (1998) points out that the effectiveness of any organization rests firmly in the hands of the people down in the trenches. If they are treated well, empowered, and respected, the company's success will follow. They are not just workers in the organization—they are the organization.*

SUMMARY

In this powerful exchange, John answers Linda's question: What would he have done differently? He shares several key gaps in the school's total curriculum package he wished he would have addressed more boldly, including reading, math, science, and the arts. He also advises her to listen to parents more, support and love the students and staff, teach and model teamwork, and build strong relationships with everyone. He stresses that he would not have been able to serve this school for ten years without a personal commitment to balance—setting professional and personal priorities and maintaining this critical focus. The first thing he advises Linda to do? Go home to her family and friends and celebrate with them this new chapter in her life.

5

REALITY

In the trenches, the soldier meets truth face to face, with no illusion as before.

John heard the phone ring inside as he finished up a woodworking project before lunch. He'd been away from school for six weeks and could not believe how relaxed he felt, how much energy he had, and how many new things he wanted to get into. Linda was on the line, and he could tell she was crying.

"John, I'm so ready for your first mentoring session. Can you come by school later today?"

"I'll be there at 4 p.m."

As John arrived, he glanced around the old school. Memories flooded his mind, and he had to refocus before he went into the principal's office. Linda burst into tears when she saw him.

"John, I feel like resigning right now. It's the second week of school, and I have so many fires to put out, I won't be able to look up until Christmas! I never dreamed it would be like this. Why didn't someone warn me?"

"OK, OK. Settle down. Just start talking and let it out. I'll listen." John remembered his first semester as principal. It had not been a piece of cake.

"Well, for starters—the president of the PTA quit on me yesterday. She said she couldn't get any volunteers to help, and the teachers didn't want to have as many night meetings this year, so she's through. The fire marshal wrote us up for having no evidence of a fire drill the first week of school. The master schedule has to be redone. My secretary has applied for a position at central office. The custodians don't get along. The parents are calling school board members over the congestion in the parking lot at afternoon dismissal. We have a lice problem in our two preschool classrooms, so I'm getting threats the local newspaper will be called if we don't get it fixed immediately. And I have three hallways of teachers who all want to do a different discipline plan. I made the mistake at our first staff meeting and invited people to implement any new ideas, and boy, did some folks take advantage of that statement."

"Wow, Linda, you have had a stressful start! Let's see, before you give up and leave town, let's just walk through some basics one at a time. For starters, tell me, what did you do to get to know all your staff and parent volunteers one-to-one?"

"One-to-one? What do you mean by 'one-to-one'? We had a kick-off celebration, and I gave the entire faculty a pep talk. We had this building looking very festive on opening day."

"That's good. Now, in the next few days, schedule meetings with every person you have on staff—including janitors, cooks, and bus drivers—and volunteer leaders too. Don't talk much, except to be friendly and open. Just welcome them into your office and sit and listen. Invite them to share what they feel is good about this school and also what needs improvement. Take notes, learn names, and find out about their families and hobbies."

"How will I find the time to do this? School has been in session for two weeks!"

"You don't have time to *not* do this, Linda. The entire year depends on how well you connect with people these first few weeks. Remember, you will be fine if you serve this school always guided by principles and relationships. After doing these interviews, maybe four a day, your notes from these conversations will be the roadmap for how you embrace this school for the next nine months."

"Just by letting people gripe?"

"No, just by letting people know you genuinely care. You do care, don't you, Linda? The parents who are complaining about head lice—put yourself in their shoes. The PTA president—no wonder she's frustrated. The custodians—they have the most unfulfilling, mundane job in the school system. Have you sat down and had a soda with them yet? Asked them what they thought about the physical plant?"

"I just assumed they did not want me hanging around. They always seem so grumpy."

"That's because they are often treated as second-class citizens, often by staff who work here in the same building."

"OK, John. I think I hear you. I've got to stop stressing over my job and start doing my job—which is to put people first and let them know I value them and their ideas, very much."

"That's the answer, Linda. I promise you, if you do the one-to-one talks, you will notice things starting to fall into place. Just focus on that for the next few days, and I'll be back around in a couple of weeks. Sooner if you need me . . . oh, one more thing, how are your daily habits going?"

"Daily habits? Well, I'm up at 5:30 a.m., home at 6:30 p.m., in bed by 10:30 p.m. So I have four hours a day for my family. I've been coming over here to catch up on Sunday afternoons. Saturdays? I'm on the couch exhausted."

"Whoa, girl! That won't do. Listen to me—this work never ends if you let it consume you. I have one other assignment for you. Simply put, you need to sleep right, exercise right, eat right, and make time for your spiritual nourishment. Try something for me. Starting tomorrow, keep a daily record of how you are addressing these four areas. For today, it's time for you to go home to your family. Remember, only two assignments: one-to-one conversations and the personal management piece as a major priority every day."

"John, thank you so much. I feel a hundred percent better already. Yes, you are right. It's 5:00 p.m., and I'm outta here. My kids will be shocked!"

In Primal Leadership, *Goleman, Boyatzis, and McKee (2002) emphasize that of all the various intellectual gifts, emotional intelligence is the most important. Thus, how we build and maintain our relationships with others makes all the difference.*

SUMMARY

As the fall semester begins, Linda is overwhelmed by the realities of the job. Various problems and issues are causing criticism as her leadership skills are tested from day one. John advises her to do two things. First, he asks her to schedule one-to-one conversations with all staff and also volunteer leaders—to simply get to know them—and to take a lot of notes as they share various suggestions and frustrations. And second, he asks her to begin keeping daily documentation of how well she is taking care of her personal balance habits—exercise, nutrition, sleep, and spiritual health.

6

NEW TEACHER BLUES

> This noble cause I have chosen is not possible to achieve—but I will try.

John had just finished his quiet time and morning walk when the phone rang.

"John, it's Linda. I can't meet today after school. Something's come up. One of my new teachers has resigned. She called me before daylight and said she just can't do this job. I'm looking for a long-term sub right now and am meeting with the superintendent in an hour!"

"OK, how about I come over first thing tomorrow morning? And do me one favor. Call that teacher and tell her not to turn in a resignation letter yet. Have her meet with us in the morning at 9:00 a.m."

When John arrived the next morning, he was given a big hug by his former secretary, Mrs. Jackson.

"Boss, thank you. You don't know what your support has meant to Linda. Let me tell you, without your pep talk a couple weeks back, I think she might have been walking out this door herself.

Since your visit, I can see a big change. And you've created a monster! She has all of us exercising and doing personal management stuff! The teachers are griping about it, but deep down—can I whisper? I think they like it!"

Linda smiled as John entered her office. "John, thank you so much for stopping by! Let me introduce you to Marcie, one of our most gifted new teachers in the district. She's had a rough month, though. I told her you wanted to see her."

"Hello, Marcie. Thank you for agreeing to come in today. Can you take a few minutes and fill me in on what's been going on in your classroom—how you feel about everything and being a first-year teacher? I'm going to mainly listen. It's good for you to get this off your chest."

"Well, I don't know what we are going to accomplish by this," Marcie answered bluntly. "I have already made up my mind that I do not want to teach anymore. But since you drove over here to try to help, sure, I'll share a few things."

Linda made a quick call on the phone to Mrs. Jackson. "Jane, no calls or interruptions, please. Give us an hour."

"It started even before the first day of school," Marcie began. "I had no idea how much paperwork and how many endless tasks were involved with teaching. I was tired by the first morning the kids arrived! Then, the first day, I realized I had inherited three little boys who have major discipline issues. In a class of twenty-four second-graders and with an aide for only two hours each morning, there is no way I can teach to the level I demand for myself."

Linda filled in, "Two of these boys have been referred for testing, and the third is already being served by our special education program. But, John, we don't have the special ed staff we really need here in this building. They are a great team, but they do not have the capacity to fulfill what is built into all the IEPs. I've asked the district for another special ed teacher, but that may take several months."

"But that's not all," Marcie continued. "That still leaves me with twenty-one other kids who need my individual attention all day long, and I just can't seem to get to all their needs. I need to have a class half this size and an aide all day long. I was able to handle large groups like this last year when I subbed, but this is different. I am responsible for teaching these kids how to read and write well, and how to fall in love with math and science."

John comforted, "I know, Marcie, I know. Every teacher I have ever worked with identifies this numbers game we play to fit budgets as the key reason they can't get more results in terms of student achievement. Is there anything else that has troubled you these first few weeks?"

"Well, frankly, a couple of parents have been quite overbearing and rude. They mean well, but their attempts to advise and help have been very insulting. Also, my mentor teacher is too busy with her own classroom here at the first of the year. We've only met to talk about these issues one time, and that was for about thirty minutes. That's partly my fault, though. I'm working on my graduate studies and taking classes two nights a week, so when she wants to talk, I usually can't meet that day after school."

John smiled, gave Marcie a hug, and simply said, "You're going to make it. I suggest you take the rest of the week off and clear your head. Let me brainstorm some with your principal here on a couple of things, but don't you dare give up yet. I bet I'll see you at Christmas and you'll have a smile on your face. Marcie, you have identified some key gaps that can help this school immeasurably. That's what leaders do—admit the realities and then help fix them. Don't walk away from your love of kids and teaching. This community needs young people like you serving in this school."

Marcie smiled, with tears in her eyes, gave Linda a long hug, and simply said, "Thank you. I will consider this."

As Marcie left, Linda shut the door, sat down, and began sobbing with her head in her hands. "I have failed that girl. I just did not know what stress she was under, until my one-to-one talk with her earlier this week. I should have had that talk the very first week of school with all of my new staff. What was I thinking?"

"Linda, you have failed no one. This level of support takes time. Marcie will be fine. Here's what I would do if I were you: I'd put together an aggressive volunteer training program, screen carefully, and then start using these folks for blocks of time in classrooms as volunteer aides. I dabbled with this tapping into the wealth of volunteer talent a little, but some teachers would pressure me to keep the 'helpers' to a minimum. I should have stayed the course. But you can follow up on my good intentions, and it will, over time, help transform this school. There are some model sites doing this around the state, and they are getting unbelievable results. Students on all levels need individual and small-group attention and tutoring. It's that simple. Schools that aggressively live by this philosophy are so much further along, and the real winners are the kids."

"This is exactly what my one-to-one parent conversations are revealing. Many of them want to help, but some feel as if we don't want them here in the building—unless they are helping us with fund-raising or with ball teams. What else do you suggest, John? I'm listening."

"While you're gearing up this parent recruitment program, develop a second strand that has your teachers doing one-to-one conversations with all parents just as you are doing with all staff. I'm not talking about the official 'parent conference' that typically has the teacher in control and in a position of threatening authority. I'm talking about now, in the first month of school, teachers taking notes and listening."

"I'll do it. It's changed my relationship with my staff so much since I started doing this with them; I know this will help my teachers to understand their parents better, and vice versa."

"Gotta go. By the way, Mrs. Jackson said you have the whole school on an exercise focus. You go, girl! How's the nutrition and rest going?"

"Eight hours of sleep every night, leaving work earlier, spending more time with my family, and eating more fruit, vegetables, and salads—with juice or water. I've cut the all-day snacking out almost entirely."

"Can you tell a difference?"

"A huge difference. I can't tell you how much!"

In The Eighth Habit, *Covey (2004) identifies a key truth for living a life of purpose. He urges the individual to find his or her voice, then focus on helping others to find their voice. We all have unique talents to give back to the world we live in. Many along the way may need us to help them see their own giftedness too, and how to best use it.*

SUMMARY

A new teacher is bombarded with first-year pressure and is ready to resign. John advises for her to take a week of rest away from school and for Linda to coordinate a schoolwide focus on recruiting and training qualified volunteers to serve as aides in the classrooms. Although he shied away from this need when he was a principal, he realizes something must be done to get this school more human resource assistance. He also recommends that all teachers schedule one-to-one "listening" chats with parents early in the semester, as Linda has been doing with staff.

7

WHAT LIES BENEATH

I looked to the distance, but danger lurked within the camp.

The passage to autumn invigorated John as he so enjoyed his projects around the house. He and his family were planning an October weekend to the mountains, and he just couldn't believe how stress-free he felt. He had scheduled to meet with Linda after school one day this week, and he was anxious to hear how Marcie was coming along.

As he checked in at the office, Mrs. Jackson just shook her head, "It's not good."

"John, so glad to see you. Have a seat." Linda looked tired and defeated as she took off her glasses and gazed out the window. John remembered that stare—he'd made it many times over the years. It's a stare of exasperation, of feeling defeated—as if to say, "There's no way out of here, is there?"

"How's Marcie?" John hoped the young woman was still teaching.

"Actually, Marcie is a success story, John. Your suggestions worked. She is getting stronger and has actually asked to serve on an advisory team of new teachers that the superintendent is putting together. She wants to share some input regarding how the district perceives what a new teacher should be able to do in year one. I think this is one of the wisest things the super has ever done. If he will listen, he may be able to develop a teacher induction model that could have impact for years to come."

"Wonderful! Linda, this concept will have awesome impact! I envy you principals as the school system dives into this type of positive change."

"Don't envy me, John. I have bigger issues. Can I just talk for a few minutes? I just need a good listener."

"OK, let it out. I won't say a word until you're completely finished."

"Well, I have been taking your advice, and one by one slowly but surely addressing culture issues. The one-to-one conversations with staff have been such a big help. And the parent involvement and relationship-building ideas are already making this place a stronger and smarter school in how we serve kids every day. But, guess what? Two of my veterans, who have been leaders in this building for years, are sabotaging everything new we try to implement."

John's shoulders sank as he realized this was going to hurt. This was his staff that he had trained and been so proud of for its maturity and understanding of team leadership.

"John, at first I thought I was being overly sensitive—a snide remark here, a sarcastic look there, a negative attitude emerging in staff meetings. But it's bigger than that. I'm talking about teacher leaders on my staff out in the community criticizing my leadership, and in the teacher's lounge encouraging younger teachers to not go along with our new parent conference plan—among other things they are trying to shoot down! I am afraid I am going to have a split faculty before Christmas! I could give you several more examples, but to save you time, let's just say that I have had several staff and even a few parents hint to me that if I don't do something fast, I am going to lose control of this ship! Please, please, please—tell me what to do!"

John remembered his first year and how it felt to be so betrayed. He remembered a good friend asking to be transferred to another school because John had moved him to a different classroom. He remembered the tension in teachers' meetings when he had to share something that was going to go against the wishes of some of the veteran "bosses" on staff. And he remembered the day he was able to let all that go and not worry about it anymore. He smiled and asked Linda if she had anything else she needed to share.

"Just that I hate supervising adults, because in many ways they are more like children than the kids are!"

"And there's your answer, Linda. Bingo!"

"What? There's my answer? Gee, thanks, John, send me your bill! You've been such a big help today!"

"No, Linda, listen to what you just said. 'They truly are like children.' We all, to varying degrees, are children in grown-up bodies. So you be the adult, and as you do with your children at home, address issues with smart psychology, and show them the way—and with a whole lot of grace and patience. Don't be their boss who is forcing them to change. Be their shepherd!"

"Be their shepherd? John, listen to me. These ladies and their growing band of followers want me to fail! They want me gone this time next year!"

"Perhaps that's what they think they want. But, Linda, what they really want is to be recognized as leaders who still have great influence in this school and community. Tell me something: what do they do best? What would you hire each of them to do if you were putting together a strong staff and had to start over?"

"If I was starting over with this school, I wouldn't hire them, period."

"I knew you were going to say that," John laughed. "But let's play this scenario out. What are they great at?"

"Well, one is known as one of the top math teachers in the county. And the other is a whiz with technology and is very good at keeping the PTA focused on student projects. She loves all the social stuff that the PTA can do during the year that highlights the kids."

"Is the math 'guru' the chair of your math committee?"

"No, I wanted someone leading that team who had a great attitude. She doesn't!"

"Well then, is the technology 'queen' the chair of your technology committee?"

"We don't call them committees anymore. But she has not been attending those team meetings. I needed her at the first of the year to serve on the calendar team."

"Why? I don't remember that she was one of my people who had a grasp on schedules and time management and things like that."

"As I think back, I'm not sure why I put her there. She seems to hate it."

"And I assume she is a PTA officer or the school's staff liaison to the PTA?"

"No, John, of course not! I'm not stupid! I wouldn't dare let her infiltrate that group and do even more damage!"

"Oh, but I'm quite sure that she already has. If that's what she loves to do—the PTA stuff—I'd say by now she's talked to many, many of the parents, and is on the phone behind the scenes helping control the PTA's plans for this year."

"So how do I get her transferred out of this building by next summer?"

John just smiled, and chuckled. "Linda, Linda, Linda. What would that prove? Would not her friends and supporters then have evidence that perhaps you too should also be removed by next summer? After all, would this not be helping prove the point that you feel these two veterans are trying to make: that you can't handle being the leader of this school? That you are the problem?"

"Yes, I guess my good intentions to protect this school could indeed backfire and get the entire community all torn up and angry—even if I was right!"

"Exactly—even if you were right. One can be right and wrong at the same time—a seldom understood principle of humanity that I learned a long time ago."

"So, John, I can't believe what I hear you saying: to compromise my principles? What about all that core values stuff you've been preaching!"

"I am not suggesting you compromise anything. I am suggesting you move past a logical answer that you know will cause a lot of hurt for this school and many, many people, and dig down deep for a best answer, a great answer, that is squarely based on your integrity and core values."

"But how?"

"Well, for starters, go back to your key principle of communication."

"I have talked, I have listened, I have brought them in to this office for the one-to-one sessions. They say one thing and do another. They have no interest in buying into the changes that are needed for this school!"

"Linda, do me a favor. One-to-one, take both of these teachers out to eat and pick their brains about all they know about this school. Ask, ask, ask. Listen, listen, listen. Then ask the math specialist to be a leader on your math team. Ask the technology specialist to be a leader on your tech team. And also ask her to be your spokesperson to the PTA when you can't attend meetings or planning sessions. As veteran leaders in this community, invite both of them to be in regular conversations with you about their insights as to how to take this school to a higher level. But also articulate to them your vision for this school and that it will take everyone working together, with all leaders on the same page."

"This will call the dogs off?"

"If you are sincere in wanting these two leaders to help you, not work against you, it may take some time, but they will come on board. But remember—see them as sheep you are shepherding. Use some child psychology. Honey is better than vinegar in these situations. Chill out, and let go of this concept that everyone must like you all the time or agree with you. Guess what? It ain't gonna happen. But if you live by your core values and principles, they will always respect you, and sooner or later, will do the right thing in what's best for the school. That's what you want to shoot for in the long haul anyway—not popularity."

"But I still think some other strategy should be initiated that somehow protects the rest of the staff and the school during this process. These two can be mean people, John."

"That's a good point. It's probably time to do a staff book study, working through it for about a month in teachers' meetings. Helping this staff continue to understand and embrace self-leadership is the key for you, in this first year, to being the true servant leader of this school. They all need to take a good look at self and make the needed adjustments. But that must start with you."

In Now, Discover Your Strengths, *Buckingham and Clifton (2001) share insights on how to help self and others identify and further develop talents and strengths, and how to better focus our work in these areas.*

SUMMARY

Linda realizes she has veteran teachers who are sabotaging her leadership. However, instead of advising her to develop a battle plan, John encourages her to take them out to eat one-to-one and truly listen to their ideas and feelings about the school—but to also share her vision for the school with them as well. Then, he recommends that Linda assign them as leaders on committees where they would have a serious interest. He sees communication, trust, and empowerment as the key variables for Linda to keep her faculty from being divided into two polarized camps. He also suggests a book study for the entire faculty on the topic of leadership.

8

TEACHING AND LEARNING

> It's not what we say, it's what we do. It's not in telling a child, it's in inspiring that child to "learn how to learn." Then, he won't need minute-by-minute instructions. He will have a world to explore.

John stopped by a couple of days later, just to make sure Linda was OK. He knew she'd been hurt by the shock of staff sabotaging her behind her back.

"How's the ship sailing today? Still on the high seas and exploring new worlds?"

"Hi, John," Linda chuckled as he entered her office. He seemed so unstressed. She longed for that freedom to be so carefree, and she wondered if she would ever be that way again. "Yes, the ship's afloat and not taking on water at the moment."

"And that's a good thing," John added as he sat down. "I was on my way out of town and just wanted to make sure you were OK after our discussion last week."

"Actually, it helped more than you know. It motivated me to get more involved in the classroom, so I have been doing 'walk-throughs' this week."

"And what have you found?"

"Well, a mixed bag. I have been pleasantly surprised in some classrooms and disappointed in others. Mainly, I just had no idea that in one school there could be such a range of teaching philosophies."

"What do you mean? Tell me more."

"Well, even with the same age groups, I found some classrooms that were very hands-on focused—with kids moving around, working with materials, doing a lot of independent learning. But right across the hall, I'd find a very structured setting, with students in rows of chairs, and the teacher up front doing quite a bit of lecturing. Or the kids were quietly doing seatwork."

"What is your preferred classroom management style, Linda?"

"I like to see a classroom with a balance of both structure and active learning. The secret for me, when I taught, was in having well-planned lessons that kept the kids engaged all day long. They weren't in activity centers all day, but they weren't glued to their chairs for vast amounts of time either. I read and told a lot of stories, we played a lot of games, did a lot of group problem solving, they played Checkers and Chess, and Scrabble and Boggle—lots of interaction and looking for answers—I saw my classroom as a wonderland of learning. For the kids, I wanted it to be as exciting as summer camp."

"What else did you find in your walk-throughs this week?"

"Not near enough hands-on science going on. Not near enough teaching of math in a way that kids could sink their teeth into it. Not near enough use of technology."

"What else?"

"Too much reading and writing as if it is painful. Not enough reading magazines, newspapers, and high-interest books. And not enough unchained writing—scripts for plays, creative stories, personal journals—I just didn't see a lot that would have been of much interest to me when I was a kid. And I absolutely loved reading and writing."

"Anything else?"

"And not near enough noise in some rooms. How can you be a community learning center, with hundreds of kids in the building all day long, and not have some vocal interaction naturally happening as part of the learning process? How do kids stand that type of environment—in their seats for hours at a time—doing written assignments? I know we adults wouldn't be able to handle it day in and day out! So why do we expect kids to?"

"No, we wouldn't like it, Linda. And the kids don't either. Far too many tell their parents later that they were bored in this grade or that classroom. But there's no easy way to fix the problems you've identified. These are teaching style issues, and some of these folks are considered master teachers and have been doing it their way for years. What do you think you should do?"

"I thought about this a lot over the weekend. I'm going to start with a threefold strategy. First, we're going to talk much more about instruction during teachers' meetings. And not just me. I'm going to have teachers sharing their best teaching tips with each other as a regular part of the agenda. Number two, we're going to look longer and harder at the whole process of how the brain learns best. Some may think this is boring or we don't have time for it, but as a school, we're going to study brain research. And finally, I'm going to show teachers exactly what I'm seeing in these walk-throughs and then have them discuss my observations in their team meetings. This will give them a chance to explain to each other why I saw what I saw. Then, I want them to visit each other's rooms and do the same thing I have been doing—observing and taking notes."

"Will they accept this bold approach?"

"Oh, don't get me wrong, John. I am not going in thinking I have all the answers. I want this to be an ongoing open discussion about how kids learn and how teachers best help them learn. Maybe that 'sit and get' all morning works for some kids. I just want all of us professionals in this building to get outside our box a little bit and do some critical thinking, ask more questions, look at our teaching habits, and see what practices bubble up as really good and hopefully see what practices are relied on less because they are no longer considered state of the art."

In Enabling Knowledge Creation, *Von Krogh, Ichijo, and Nonaka (2000) reverse the age-old paradigm that places the emphasis on managing the information that is shared with students, sharing instead innovative strategies of how to unlock tacit knowledge. Learning is not about spewing out facts or the pages covered in a book. Learning is a transformation—a thirst to know more—and is always taking place, throughout life.*

SUMMARY

Linda wisely begins to spend more time in her teachers' classrooms and discovers that some, but not enough, engaging teaching is going on that addresses the variety of student learning styles. She is disappointed that depth of knowledge seems to be ignored in favor of covering a lot of material. She is especially troubled over the lack of independent reading and creative writing time, and the lack of higher-level math and science. She is also concerned about her school's limited treatment of the arts. She decides to address the whole issue of instructional effectiveness with a three-pronged approach: in-depth instructional discussions in teachers' meetings; a schoolwide study of brain research and how children learn; and teachers modeling and learning from each other in peer-observation classroom visits.

9

GROWTH PLANS

The coach worked his team into the night, not resting on the success of yesterday.

The middle of the fall season brought with it a nostalgia as John thought back over the years. The cool winds reminded him of the long, hard winter that was around the corner. He had always cherished the coziness of this time of year at school—when everyone settled in and had several months of work that was not so distracted by outside interests. He had always wondered why, at least in the warm-weather months, more schools did not experiment with a "half-day classroom" model. Highly focused morning academic classes with afternoon arts, clubs, and other activities would certainly be welcomed by the kids—and parents too, who would like to have the family home in the evenings instead of the endless running to and fro.

As John drove to Heritage to visit with Linda, he wondered why he had not pursued this concept, at least as a pilot. Perhaps the school board would have let him try it for a year or two. The whole idea of the traditional 8 a.m. to 3 p.m. format, without trying new creative options that better suited how kids of various ages learn best, had always troubled him.

"John, come in! So good to see you! I have some encouraging news!"

Linda was beaming and much more relaxed and at peace than John had seen her all semester. "I have been doing what you suggested—turning negatives into positives, lemons into lemonade. One-to-one conversations and empathetic listening, followed by empowerment, has brought the staff around, and I don't think I have a civil war going on anymore."

"Well, congratulations! You have made my week! Sounds like you have helped turn the tide. How has it happened so fast?"

"Well, your book study idea was brilliant. We are doing these in small groups all over the building and then discussing them in weekly staff meetings. I am asking others to facilitate these staff sessions, instead of me being up front and center stage all the time. This really shifts the leadership and responsibility to the entire staff team. I don't feel like it's all on my shoulders anymore."

"Wise move, Linda. This is a great example of 'less is more.' Leadership is not about pulling and controlling the sled, so to speak. It is more about equipping it so you can let it go."

"Well, I have been amazed at how the culture around here is changing, as you said it would. I just have one question. With all of this leading by 'giving up,' I sometimes shudder to think what could happen if a pocket of power would rise up and start taking the school in the wrong direction. Strong-willed teachers, parents, even well-intended school board members—am I not putting myself in a very vulnerable position here, by opening up the can of worms that everyone's ideas are good ones, and everyone is a leader? Doesn't that lead to chaos if some would choose to take advantage with selfish motives or hidden agendas?"

"That's where your leadership is critical. You must keep folks focused on the vision—turning this place into a great school that puts kids first every day and with each staff member taking pride in personal development."

"Well, I have been doing that already, haven't I?"

"Have you? What do the individual growth plans look like?"

"Well, I know they were updated by everyone in April when you met with each person at the end of the last school year and worked on evaluations, and I assume the staff all know to look at them as they plan their training needs for this year."

"Oh, but they won't, Linda. Do you pull your growth plan out and look at it?"

Linda grinned sheepishly. "I don't have one. The superintendent asked me to send him a draft that he would send feedback on, but I was going to wait until Thanksgiving break."

"Don't feel bad," John continued. "But I guarantee that your staff hasn't followed up on theirs either—other than to take some required professional development this summer. But that's different than a personal growth plan. A personal growth plan should be very detailed and specific. It's a one- or two-page self-assessment that includes input from the supervisor and should guarantee an employee is growing and developing all year long."

"So if I sit down with each employee between now and Thanksgiving, and we talk about their IGP for this school year, I am holding them accountable to that plan now—not just in April when I do the dreaded evaluation."

"Exactly. What good is an evaluation, really, if we only work on it once a year every spring? It's a dreaded ritual that has little value to the school or the employee."

"Oh, John, here we go. I'm afraid teachers will resent this, and the trust I've been building will be ruined. Shouldn't I wait and implement the IGP model you're talking about this next year?"

"You could. That's what I did for several years. I put off the real discussions about specific areas each staff person could be working on to improve themselves as professional educators."

"And you still built a great school! You were known as one of the best school leaders this region has ever known."

"But how much greater could we have been, Linda? And all those teachers did not grow under my mentoring as they could have, because I didn't know any better. Until three years ago, when I started taking the IGP and evaluation process as a twelve-month, ongoing accountability model that I and all of my staff had to live by, we flew by the seat of our pants. That's no way to run a school if you really want each staffer, including you, to grow month by month."

"OK. Where do I even start?"

"Simply talk about strengths and also areas that need more attention. Do both. Never just compliment or just target weaknesses. Engage each staff person in honest self-assessment about where they are and where they want to be in the coming months. Write it down, revisit it before Christmas, and then get each person the training, mentoring, or other help they need. They won't turn on you if you care enough to hold them accountable by providing ongoing support. They will respect you, and you will be helping to turn average teachers into good teachers, and good teachers into great teachers."

"And what about the poor teachers?"

"I never hired any poor teachers. I took as long as it took, but I can honestly say that I always hired the best that was available—every time."

"But sometimes, the logical choice is someone from the community who deserves their turn. Maybe a sub who has been good to us. Maybe a former student of this school."

"Linda, I know. The variables can get complicated. But if you want to build a great school, you must build a great staff. It's that simple. I trust you will know what to do the next time a vacancy occurs."

"But feelings get hurt, John, when someone is passed over."

"And kids get hurt, sometimes permanently, when the classroom is not being supervised by a competent, well-trained teacher. This is about kids, Linda. What you and your staff do here every day—every minute—is about kids, and giving them every opportunity to excel in life."

In Formula 2 + 2, *Allen and Allen (2004) offer a simple growth plan model that allows the supervisor and the employee to have ongoing and routine discussions about what is going well and what needs more attention. This process allows for continued coaching and feedback—a much more helpful approach than the traditional annual evaluation model.*

SUMMARY

John coaches Linda on the importance of the individual growth plan for all staff, and then ongoing follow-up. He admits that without the regular feedback—targeting areas for improvement and also complimenting areas of strength—the annual evaluation is almost useless. Linda is hesitant to implement such a model because she wonders how the weaker teachers will react. John reminds her that her role is to help build the best staff that can be assembled, and that anything less is cheating the students.

10

THE INTRAMURAL LEAGUE

The child thirsts to kick the ball and run with the others on the field of dreams.

John did not push to keep visiting Linda every two weeks. He could tell she was growing as a leader and did not want to overwhelm her with so many new ideas that she lost her focus. But she would have it no other way. She had him on her calendar for twice a month, if not more. And when the first November visit rolled around, she had a doozy for him that could potentially rock the school, community, and entire school district.

"John, tell me how to fix our athletic program. I love the fact that it is run by volunteers. The elementary athletic boosters' league in this county is very strong, and I appreciate how organized it is and how the responsibility is taken off the schools. But I had a sobbing mother in here yesterday who explained to me that her son was cut from our fifth-grade basketball team! Unless I'm wrong, I don't even think we're allowed to 'cut' players from clubs at this level, correct?"

"Well, yes and no," explained John. "If the boosters are running the league, as parents do Little League baseball in the summer and with lots of other community leagues, the school has no jurisdiction. But I thought the boosters worked that out a couple of years back, when we turned the operation of elementary basketball over to them. I didn't know they were allowing any cutting of players."

"Well, the mom said it's disguised. An 'all-star' team is selected to represent the school on road trips outside of the district, and the rest of the kids are told they will get to play on Saturdays in the county league. However, she said that her son was told by his coach that he should try another sport and that he wouldn't get to play much at all because he was so little. So she took that to mean he was being told to go home."

"Linda, I thought all the kids were divided up equally on however many teams were needed, and all played equal amounts of time every Saturday from December to March. It's a developmental league and is supposed to be for fun for any child in our school who wants to play. Who is the coach?"

"He's a new guy, just moved back home from college. I called him at home to make sure the mother wasn't confused, and he pretty much told me that he was going to get the league to change some of its policies, because he could not take the best players to the level they needed to be if he had to 'baby-sit'—as he phrased it—every kid who could pick up a basketball."

"Did you explain that this is an elementary school, not high school or college?"

"Yes, and he replied that in college, intramurals were for the lesser athletes, and that's what we needed if we wanted to give every child in the school an opportunity to play. He was only interested in taking talented kids to the max, to help them get scholarships to college to play ball as he had done."

"Then start an intramural league."

"What? John, we have over three hundred kids in this school!"

"Linda, remember: it's in our school's strategic plan for this year anyway. Offer it to all students and let your PTA coordinate it, but with you having direct oversight of the policies and details."

"What about the boosters' Saturday league?"

"Oh, let them do what they are doing. Just contact the league president immediately, and let him know your new coach is planning to bust up the true spirit of their league. I know the man—he'll take care of it. But I would also tell him that you are expanding their concept and offering a Friday evening recreational league for your school."

"But will I have enough kids to run such a league?"

"Are you kidding? They'll come out in droves! If the PTA will recruit volunteers and referees for you, this will not be hard to do. They could even sell refreshments and this could be their key fund-raiser for the entire year. Perhaps this will keep your students from having to sell candy bars all fall!"

"So, really, we're not limiting any other sports programs. We're just offering an alternative for all those kids who just want to wear a basketball jersey and play on the court in a real live game."

"Exactly. And their moms and dads can watch them from the stands, with the opportunity to help coach them, and this school can be known as a school that offers after-school recreation opportunities like no other!"

"Yes! Why stop with basketball? We could offer volleyball, then soccer, then some intramural track and field. And next fall, perhaps even softball!"

"Yes, the sky's the limit. Why not?"

"We will only be limited by the variable of how well we recruit volunteer coordinators and coaches for each sport. And if it's only one game a week, without all that practice and travel, I know I can find parents to do this."

"Linda, can you imagine the excitement? The kids will absolutely love this!"

"You know, regarding some other times to exercise and just 'free play,' I can see this leading to us opening the gym Monday through Thursdays, right after school for a couple of hours."

"If you, your staff, and your parents truly believe in what's best for kids, this will be one of the best programs ever started in this town—maybe in this state!"

"I'm going to do it, John! *I am going to do it!*"

"You go, girl. Keep me posted!"

In The Boundaryless Organization, *Ashkenas, Ulrich, Jick, and Kerr (2002) urge organizations to break the chains of organizational structure, thus opening the door to the creation of new models that better meet the needs of all stakeholders.*

SUMMARY

Basketball season brings with it the usual headaches, and Linda is frustrated when a parental complaint reveals that the elementary league is not as much instructional as it is overly competitive. When a student is cut from his team by an overzealous coach, John persuades Linda to recruit volunteers to create a weekend intramural league, open to all students and focused on participation, play, and fun.

11

CORE VALUES

It is that which I think about, I do, and that which I believe in,
I die for.

John returned the week before Thanksgiving, and Linda was just bubbling over how well the parents and the entire community had embraced her intramurals model.

"Core values, Linda. This whole thing is about core values. Matter of fact, every new project you've started this fall semester is about core values."

"What do you mean, John? I'm just listening to people and supporting their good ideas."

"Yes, but it's more than that. You're helping Heritage to find its northern compass. You're helping this school and entire community to live its mission, to believe in its vision, and to use all of its resources to put relationships and kids first. Many organizations talk about their core values, but few actually live by them on a daily basis—no matter what."

"Well, I must say, the core values that drive this school are certainly very visible everywhere I look. You did a great job, John, of reminding people what this school is all about. They're on your school stationery, on the wall out in the front lobby, down the hallways, and in the classrooms."

"Yes, and I did that for a reason. I wanted the entire Heritage community to embrace them, to breathe them, to live them! Frankly, it's largely a waste of time to go to the trouble to identify core values if you don't share them. That's why many organizations don't. They know they can't walk the talk."

"I'm curious, John. Let's go down the Heritage list of core values. So you're saying not every school truly puts kids first? Not every school stresses relationship as the key to everything else working well? Not every school believes in people over profit? Not every school embraces the community around it? Not every school is committed to ongoing growth and improvement? John, may I be honest with you? I find this hard to believe."

"Linda, it's not that a school, a board, or any organization sets out on purpose to not live by the highest of principles, driven by core values that are noble and good. It's just that, like individuals who are not good at prioritizing what really is important in life, an organization can lose its way."

"Well, I can think of a company or two that I've read about that had obviously lost its way! The news is full of corporate scandals that were caused by human carelessness and lack of being driven by principles."

"Exactly! It's so, so sad. Do you think these organizations were driven by healthy core values that placed people over profits, relationships over numbers and data, and the common good over selfish gain?"

"Obviously, John, they lost their northern compass, as you say, somewhere earlier in their development as a corporation."

"Yes! Somewhere, they wandered down the wrong path. Maybe it was careless leadership by one or several people, maybe it was a board that did not know how to hold itself and its members accountable, maybe it was 'not knowing what they didn't know' about a lot of things. But, always, the meltdown and ruin of an organization can be traced back to lack of conscious living day to day by a healthy set of core values that are relentlessly believed in and followed. If noble principles don't drive the organization, eventually, the organization crumbles, or at least it is mediocre."

"Are you saying a lot of schools are crumbling or at least mediocre?"

"Linda, I am just saying that Heritage will only be as good as you, your staff, and the entire community believe it can be, by staying true to the core values you referred to earlier. When I left, and later on when you move on, when teachers retire, when families move out of the community, when kids move on to the middle school—what's left that is healthy and good is not just the memory of those who have gone. It's the timeless principles that will live on and on, down through the ages. That's why they have to be visible, learned, believed in, and practiced—every day."

"John, I'm starting to see how it all relates—and the role I play. In a sense, I am the gatekeeper, the shepherd, the role model. My time is not to only be spent on 'busy-ness' and endless 'putting out fires.' It is to be focused on helping everyone who is a part of Heritage in any way to learn and practice these basic core values. And I can best do that by modeling them myself."

"Linda, you've got it! And you know what? You do this day by day, and soon there will be fewer fires to put out and less busywork that has little connection with the priorities of that day, month, or school year."

"But what about all the stuff that gets passed down to us by the top or by well-intended partners? I know just in the last two weeks there have been three new projects started in our district that are all great ideas, but I just don't have the staff on board to complete these projects at this stage of the fall semester."

"Then simply tell the district office what you told me. You will need more staff or it will have to wait until next semester or the next school year."

"Won't they get mad?"

"I hope not. But if they do, good may still come from the tension. They will understand better what your school is about and what you truly need in terms of support from the district level."

"And what about when other civic groups or agencies come in and want to offer a service or give us more resources to provide added instruction to our kids? These are all wonderful offers of support, but sometimes, they just add to the confusion and stress. My teachers hate to see one more packet of information in their mailboxes. It just overwhelms them once the school year has begun."

"The same answer is appropriate: 'Thanks for the offer, and we will consider this next semester or next summer'—especially if you also have the added staff or people support to help pull it off."

"And this works with staff conflict, parents, kids with bad attitudes as well—just quote the core value and tell them to have a nice day?"

"If you and the entire school are living the core values daily, it does get easier and easier to start the conversations by stating the core values. Many times this does indeed diffuse the situation and helps the individuals involved see the unselfish, supportive role they are supposed to play."

"Wow, I could get used to this, John. You have explained that there is indeed a better way to live this school life, without so much stress and the feeling of being overwhelmed. I am changing the agenda of my teachers' meeting this week. I am going to slow down and just have a 'heart to heart' with my staff about our core values. I have been pushing them too hard in some areas that are just not a big part of what this school needs to be focused on here in November, or what we can handle."

"Linda, just remember—sometimes, less is more. Sometimes your daily calendar needs to be free enough so you have plenty of time to walk around the building and chat with people, as well as just to sit in your office for a few minutes and think. Sometimes, it's better just to make sure all your staff feels supported, and with the time and resources to do what they are now doing well. If 'students first' is truly the key value this school lives by, this place needs to be a learning center with a daily rhythm of student, staff, and community interaction. If it seems more like a shopping mall, with the hectic feeding frenzy that goes with it, then help these people to find the true magic of 'school.'"

In The Moral Imperative of School Leadership, *Fullan (2003) challenges the education community to realize the critical role principals play in school transformation, and he challenges principals to accept the role of moral leader of the school—charting a course that truly puts children first every day.*

SUMMARY

As the school year is shaping up into one of bold change and renewal, John reminds Linda that such momentum is not just happening by chance. Instead, it is taking place because the school's core values and vision are being taken seriously. Linda is beginning to understand that organizational principles and beliefs drive so much more than just the day-to-day activities and that the role she plays is crucial.

12

ONE CHILD

> They come to us in masses, bus load after bus load. And we ask ourselves, "How can we help the ones who have no love at home?" Their souls are barren, their hearts scarred—their future hangs on by a thread. Yet we try—because every now and then, one of them makes it out of the abyss. And if we can do it for one, we can do it for a whole lot more.

Linda sat staring at her computer, not able to go to the outer office where she was to greet a reporter who had called to do a story on her school. She asked her secretary to reschedule for tomorrow and called John.

"I came as fast as I could. You said one of your students is in trouble? Have you called the police?"

"Yes, and they were very helpful. But they can't guarantee that the child is going to be OK."

"Child abuse?"

"Yep." Linda turned away to stare vacantly out the window.

"I'm sure your staff has done all they can do, Linda. You'll have to let it go."

"Let it go?" She glared at John as she rushed to the coat rack. "Let it go, John? This little baby, five years old, was found by the bus driver this morning looking for food in a garbage can. Apparently, she'd been left there in that shack of a home all night. Mom was out painting the town red on a drunken binge. Dad has disappeared and no one knows where he is. Rumor has it he's one of the main drug dealers in the county."

"Where are you going?"

"John, I'm going to the courthouse to get more answers as to why this child is still in that home. We've called and called over these past few weeks to report that something was not right. She's just a baby, John. She comes to school in dirty clothes, with an odor, and dirty hands. She's not been bathed for days! We're just lucky she wasn't killed last night or froze to death out in the cold. Or died of hunger. This is madness. Our county's stray dogs have a better chance of making it than innocent little children like this—being raised by parents who don't have the skills to take care of themselves, much less the basic human instincts to raise children!"

"OK, OK. You're right. But sit down and collect yourself for a minute. You talk—I'll just listen."

Linda fell back into her chair and just starred emptily into space. She felt so defeated, so helpless, so a part of the system that was so broken it made her stomach turn. She wanted out. She wanted to be a nurse or a missionary or a judge. Somehow, she wanted to be able to do more to help all these kids in her school who weren't being raised by loving, competent parents.

"John, I've changed my mind. I'm not going down to the courthouse. They are as handcuffed by the system as we are here at school. I'm going to my pastor, and I'm asking him to take this matter to the churches here in this community. They will know what to do. Somehow, they will find a way to get this child a warm bed, fresh new clothes, and enough food. And maybe they can get her parents some counseling, maybe even get them to take some responsibility—or admit to themselves they can't handle it and need help in raising their kids."

"Sounds like a good 'next step' to me, Linda. Perhaps this plan will benefit other kids in this school too, who live in abusive homes. How many would you say are standing out there in the cold every morning, waiting for the bus, and without the basic support and love they need from those they live with?"

"Oh, at least 10 percent of our student population. So, just here at Heritage, probably at least thirty kids who are living in unnecessary poverty and in conditions that are not fit for any human—either physically, emotionally, or both."

"Will this community's churches be able to handle that type of reality?"

"Well, if they can't, they're sure preaching a message of hope and love of neighbor they don't really understand, don't you think? And in some ways, as a school here, so do we. We sure talk the talk about every child chasing his or her dreams. But are we really helping these thirty, John, to even have a chance at the American dream?"

"Linda, I can just say this: you are trying. It may not seem like it, but that makes a huge difference. Some of them will make it. Just keep not letting up until more and more of them make it. That's the key."

"John, did you have this many of what I call 'the lost children' when you were here?"

"Yes, I'm sure we did. After a while, I just chose to look the other way. I guess I let the broken system break me, too."

In Overcoming the Dark Side of Leadership, *McIntosh and Rima (1997) address the reality of careless, weak, and sometimes immoral leadership tendencies. All leaders struggle with accountability issues. When not dealt with and corrected, hurt to self and others will result.*

SUMMARY

Linda faces the stark reality of poverty, parental neglect, and child abuse. Determined to not let one of her students be lost to a world that seems to have no answers for how to protect the helpless children in our society, she turns to the churches in her community for assistance. John admits that over the years he had become numb to the truth, and that several students a year most likely had lived in substandard conditions at home.

13

HALFWAY

I would lie down, but there's much to do and still many to care for.

John returned for a final fall semester visit in the middle of December, and Linda was up to her neck with Christmas celebrations, involving the entire school in a campaign to focus on those in the community who needed to have the opportunity to celebrate the season. Kids were visiting nursing homes, donating presents for a local hospital, and engaged in a schoolwide thematic unit on the historical impact of Christianity on civilization.

"John, as we started visiting our core values more intently around the building in the past few weeks, we realized one key principle we live by around here is truth. One of my teachers said she had always wanted to teach the history of Christianity, since it has been the driving religion of our country since its inception. So we're doing it. Our kids love it! I have been shocked at how many of them had no clue why Christmas is an international holiday celebrated around the world."

"What did your superintendent say?"

"He said that not teaching kids the whole of history is censorship and a form of rewriting the history books. So as long as we don't promote our personal feelings about Christianity, what we are doing is no different than studying the pyramids of Egypt or the writings of Plato and Socrates. He says it is extremely dangerous for a society to sanitize its culture and pretend key aspects have not existed, or don't still exist, that have been cornerstones of that society's development."

"Is your thematic focus including the actual philosophy and teachings of Jesus?"

"Of course it is, just as we include the variety of quotes and philosophies found in our history books from the many other figures who have shaped our world. What helped us realize how we had been shorting our kids of the whole story was when we realized they were learning much more about Adolf Hitler in school than they were the man from Nazareth who helped transform the world. We realized we did not have a comprehensive balance."

"You make such a good point. Well, as you wrap up the first half of the school year, what are your overall impressions?"

"I am tired but also excited. I think we have had a very focused fall semester and have dug deeper into what we really need to be about as a school. Relationships are growing, trust is happening, and we definitely monitor how we are making our decisions based on our core values more often. John, I owe so much of how this first semester went to you and your wisdom. You have been a lifesaver!"

"No, Linda, I have been a good listener and perhaps a mentor. But you have been the servant leader who has helped this school move right on to its next level. I am so proud of you! I'm very much at peace that my decision to step aside last summer was a good one."

"I have one question. After the holiday break, when we roll back in here in January, what should I expect? Is it calm during the winter? Do I sit back and wait until the spring for us to plan for next year?"

"Very proactive thinking, Linda. You're getting it in terms of being the visionary shepherd of the school. Actually, most schools do as you suggest. Winter is a time of settling in. The kids aren't as busy with evening and outside hobbies and activities. The snow season causes some delays and cancellations. But, on the other hand, it can be the calm before the storm. When the spring hits, there is way too much to do in a short amount of time in wrapping up one year and planning for another. It can be very chaotic, and hurt feelings and poor decisions run at their highest level in the late spring."

"Well, I certainly want to avoid that. I remember as a teacher how I hated those end-of-year committee meetings and deciding about allocation of budgets, moving of rooms, who went where, and so on. You're right. It was very stressful and many times ineffective."

"Well, one way to eliminate that is to just keep your staff in think-tank mode all year long. Don't wait until spring."

"How do I do that? We don't receive our new budget formula from the district office until March or April."

"No, but you can already be doing ongoing planning for what the priorities are for this spring semester, and that will then propel the school right into summer and next fall. In other words, much like your ongoing growth plans with staff, do this for the school as a whole. Remember what I told you, when I started doing this—holding us all accountable to look at our strategic plan, and updating it as needed throughout the year. It changed our school forever."

"Well, I guess that would start with setting a proactive schoolwide agenda for the spring semester. This would help all of us to stay focused on priorities and not wander here and there suddenly trying to fit everything in near the end of school."

"Yes, but before that, simply do a midyear self-assessment with all staff, students, parents, and other partners. Create a short survey: 'what did we do well, what can we spend more time on, what are our needs for the future.' Distribute it to all of your stakeholders now, before the break. You will then have an unbelievable momentum going into second semester, based on some wonderful feedback."

"So you're suggesting that we take a thorough look inside now, instead of waiting until May? Not just set a priority agenda and update our master calendar, but make sure our perceptions about what is most important for the rest of this school year are accurate?"

"Yes. Why not? It will only help all of you to be even more focused on the most critical priorities, based on ensuring that your core values drive everything you do."

"This could result in a lot of negative comments, John. I don't need that before Christmas! I've earned a break without worry."

"I don't think it will. I think you all have had a great fall. But don't be afraid of people being honest with you from their perspectives. Embrace their suggestions for improvement as the most important of all the feedback you get. That's how an organization truly moves from good to great—you absolutely must look inside and address any and all issues that have been overlooked and that could grow into bigger problems."

"But I thought all of this for the current year was in the strategic plan developed last year?"

"Yes, there were wonderful ideas in that plan. But, Linda, look at this fall semester. Look at all the things we've talked about that needed fine-tuning or more attention. A strategic plan that really works is an ongoing, living, breathing organism that always adapts and adjusts, and is always based on needs, priorities, data, and self-reflection. It is to be used as a tool for vision and focus but also for very smart implementation of the right strategies. It does nothing in itself except to sit on a shelf and collect dust."

"So I can do a midyear self-assessment of this entire school, community and all, and that can help me zero in on the second semester? And the district office will not accuse us of straying from our strategic plan?"

"No! They will be thrilled that you have your school even addressing strategic planning and taking it seriously here in December! Remember, fine-tuning and tweaking is often all that is needed. But without constant self-assessment, that look in the mirror, you will find after a few years that as the principal you see the school trapped in its same habits and paradigms, accepting weaknesses and gaps that have been there for a long time. There's no reason to operate with such a self-destructive process."

"OK, John. I'll do it. When I see you in January, I'll have a midyear report for you, based on feedback from all our stakeholders. I'll call it my 'state of the school,' and it'll include the three areas you have suggested: 1) what is going well, 2) what needs more attention, and 3) vision for the future."

In Prioritize!, *Calhoun and Jeffrey (2005) stress that too often organizations don't plan well because basic priorities are not addressed first. Thus, long and cumbersome strategic plans sit on the shelf, largely ignored. They recommend short but powerful strategic plans that address the reality of what needs to be done to improve now—and then actually doing it.*

SUMMARY

As the halfway point of year one approaches, Linda stays true to her focus on core values, and helps Heritage embrace the study of the Christian movement during the Christmas season—thus preventing the school from censoring out a vital part of history and Christianity's impact on the American culture. When she asks John what she should be doing in preparing for second semester, he advises her to conduct a midyear school self-assessment now—including feedback from students, staff, parents, and other stakeholders. This proactive data-gathering and look inside will then allow Heritage to make adjustments and further improvements immediately, instead of waiting until summer or longer.

14

CULTURE!

> When I walk into a place, I know at once if I am among friends or strangers.

The Christmas season was snowy, and when January rolled around, it kept snowing. John waited a few days into the new year and then stopped by for a visit with Linda on a snow day. She was there working, but the rest of the school was home due to slick roads.

"Hi, John. Come in. I was just ready to call you. I have some interesting data for you to look at from our midyear self-assessment. With all this snow these past few days, I feel for the first time since I took this job that I am halfway caught up."

"Super! Yes, I remember well this season of the year. It's certainly a great time for the principal to get to some of the things that are hard to pay attention to when everything is in high gear. Well, I'm curious—tell me, how did the surveying go?"

"Overall, I'm pleased. The bottom line: the kids feel safe and nurtured here. But interestingly, many of our best students say we don't challenge them enough in the classroom. They say they're bored much of the time. They also wish we had more variety in our curriculum, especially in the arts."

"What did your parents say?"

"Our parents loved the focus on conferences with teachers back in the fall and give us high marks for starting the intramural program. They only wish we offered more clubs and other after-school activities for the kids. They feel our facility has all kinds of potential to be used by the community more as well."

"What did the community partners say?"

"They think we're a great school but really don't know very much about us at all. We have a lot of work to do in the area of marketing our programs and successes to the larger community. One businessman said he had made a large donation to a regional college and would rather have had his money stay here close to home, but he just did not know where and what to donate to. That almost made me cry!"

"And your staff?"

"Well, the teachers miss you, John—a lot. It has been very hard to follow a legend, but I knew that was going to happen going in, so I am OK with it. This is an awesome opportunity, and I know the role I am supposed to play—to take the work you started here to an even higher level and not worry about who gets the credit."

"Don't sell yourself short. You're getting lots of things done I was not able to put in place. The acceptance of you, and allowing me to fade into the background, is a natural transition that will indeed happen. Just keep loving these folks. What else did the surveying reveal?"

"Well, the clerical staff, custodians, and cooks all pretty much feel things are fine. But they hint that they do not feel as they are equal players on the team."

"How do the teachers feel about this perception?"

"They basically don't even notice it. They are covered up with paperwork and the usual pressure, and many of them just want to get the school day over with and go home."

"What do you think you should do?"

"John, I know what I'm going to do. This semester, we are putting people first—every day, all over the school, and in the community. May we never let a custodian's birthday go by without a big celebration or a bus driver take a group of our kids on a field trip without us showing appreciation from the heart in a special way. Some days, we may just have to stop classes and join together in the gym for a celebration—or in the cafeteria—and certainly more often on the intercom. And we're going to fill our hallways with what this school is really about. I'm covering these dull light colors—that make us look like a hospital—with real people stuff. You know, one of our teachers was recognized last month by the school board for her contribution to a state department committee. We should have honored her here for such an accomplishment. I'm still going to do it when everyone returns to school, and in a big way too."

"And what about the kids who say they are bored?"

"I'm going to the community for volunteers, and we're no longer watering down the school day for our brightest kids. If we have to, we'll send them to the gym or cafeteria with a tutor, put them on independent projects and research in our library or computer lab, assign them to working with our younger kids for parts of the day, let them design these student clubs the parents are asking for—surely we can think outside the box and engage these kids more so they are inspired by this school—not bored by it!"

"The tapping into the community for volunteer tutors and mentors is an awesome idea. It will take time to identify them and do the background checks, but wow, will it be worth it! Now be prepared, some teachers will resist this. But keep reminding them that Heritage is about core values. If outside resources can make this a better learning center for the students, then that overrides a few on staff not wanting to be forced out of their comfort zones."

"And, John, regarding the marketing of our school, I am going to name a task force with representatives from our student body, staff, and community, and let them take over this project. Together, they'll have all kinds of ideas and know how to implement them."

"And the suggestions to open up the school more? How can that be fixed? The staff does have other lives."

"John, if you knew how many times this year I have heard people say that they wish this community had a YMCA or something for folks to do in the evening. So, guess what: I'm going to the next town council meeting and I'm going to ask them if they want to use our building after school and on weekends for all kinds of community activities. As I thought about this, I had to ask myself: 'why should I and the custodians keep the keys to this place and lock it down, except for when we have classes during the day or a ball game in the evening?' I just have one question: will the school board let me do this?"

"The old board of a few years back wouldn't have heard of such a sharing of the district's facilities. But your timing is perfect, Linda. With our current superintendent, he and the current board want us opening our doors to our partners. There may be some details that need to be worked out regarding the extra upkeep and utilities, but they will not be an issue. You're right on target. This town needs to be more connected with social activities and recreational options. This school may just be the answer."

"And wouldn't this 'opening of our doors' be considered a marketing strategy?"

"Oh my goodness, yes! You put this in motion, and in a few months, you will have people coming out of the woodwork wanting to donate in various ways to help the school."

"So, John, you mean I could start a drive to raise funds to add to our playground, to purchase more science, art, music, and P.E. equipment? To pay for more cultural field trips or to bring more culture here to the school?"

"It's pretty much guaranteed, Linda. If you develop this carefully and do it right, the community will fall in love with this school as never before. The dots will be connected, and the partnership will be a win-win for all. And, if I remember, another key priority in this year's strategic plan was to attempt to get all parents involved in at least one service project for the school. This new open-door philosophy will definitely help with implementing that part of the plan."

"And, John, I had been putting another new project off, not knowing how on earth we would actually do it. Remember from last spring? This year's plan also called for a huge nature center, including a vegetable garden. Realistically, when would the staff have time to pull this off? But a group of volunteers could put some thought into this and really develop something special for our students—an outdoor learning center that could also be shared and enjoyed by the entire community."

"I don't see why not, Linda. With this philosophy of welcoming more partners to volunteer time and talents with the school, the possibilities are endless."

In The 360 Leader, *Maxwell (2005) emphasizes that leaders need to know how to lead up, across, and down. He adds that the leader at the top is only one piece of the total picture of how leadership is taking place throughout the organization all the time. So, a wise leader will not hold back all this talent—but instead set it free and watch it multiply the health and effectiveness of the organization.*

SUMMARY

The midyear school self-assessment revealed a general satisfaction from stakeholders but also several gaps. Students wanted more challenging classes and more variety in the curriculum. Parents saw a need for more extracurricular and club offerings. Classified staff often felt unappreciated. And the community did not know nearly as much about the school as Linda had assumed. So, now that she has her priorities for improvement, she shares with John a plan of engagement and appreciation extended to all partners that will open the doors of Heritage to the community as never before.

15

GRACE, WITH ACCOUNTABILITY

It is not our place to judge, but it certainly is our place to care enough to teach each other that actions have consequences.

As the first of February rolled around, John could tell that Linda was much more self-confident, more self-controlled, and more comfortable with her role as the leader of her school. So he was not all that surprised when she shared with him that she was preparing to dive into a very controversial issue that could have serious ramifications for her career.

"John, we have a parent volunteer here at Heritage—actually, the vice president of our PTA, who does not seem to live the life he pretends he does to all of us here. I need to know what you would do if you found out some very unethical stuff about one of your key parents and one of the school's biggest supporters."

"Uh-oh, sounds serious, Linda. Well, since I've been preaching ethics and core values from day one in our chats this year, you better fill me in more if you can."

"Well, let me put it this way. I have a parent who is having an open affair here in the community. We have some PTA funds missing, and he was the last person who had access to any loose change the night we had our fall festival here at the school. And if that's not enough, two of my teachers strongly suspect he physically abuses his children. We know for certain that he verbally abuses them—we've experienced that in the parking lot after ball games that did not go his way in terms of how well his kids played. But we suspect there's more than just emotional abuse."

"Linda, do I know this man?"

"Unfortunately, we all know him. He's one of our key civic leaders—a so-called pillar of the community."

"Oh boy, what a nightmare!"

"Yes, indeed, what a nightmare! Here I've been emphasizing core values and integrity to this staff, our students, and the entire community as what we are about every day at Heritage, and now a key leader and influencer is just throwing all of this right back in our faces—whether he realizes it or not."

"What do you think you should do about this, Linda?"

"I think I know what I must do. But before I answer your question, John, did you ever have something like this come up that was right in the middle of the school community?"

"Yes, I did. And even worse, in that instance it was a teacher."

"What happened, and how did you fix it?"

"I won't use names, but I had a young teacher who had a substance abuse problem. Eventually, his addiction to alcohol caused him to routinely show up late for work. And, a couple of times, he had slurred speech in social settings here at school—ball games, things like that. I checked our school system's policy manual, which clearly stated that an employee could be dismissed for activity that was detrimental to students under his or her care. I then confronted him about his problem."

"Did he deny it?"

"At first he did, but I had been wise enough to remember to document the specific occasions on which I or others had witnessed his disease spilling over into his work. When I showed him the documentation, he stopped making excuses and listened. I put him on a corrective action plan, which basically was a 'strike three' model, and told him that he currently had already passed strike one. He agreed to seek professional treatment immediately for his condition. He and I met every two weeks for the rest of the year to discuss in detail his job performance and what needed to be worked on to help him become a better teacher and leader in the school community."

"And did he respond to this accountability and overcome his careless drinking?"

"Well, for an alcoholic, total abstinence is crucial. He was able to stop drinking cold turkey, but the damage had been done to his personal life. His wife left him, and the last I heard, he was living in another state, working in a different profession."

"Would the school district have let you go the extra mile with him and keep him on as a teacher?"

"Yes, as long as he was alcohol free and clean of his disease spilling over into the school community."

"If he had still remained a problem drinker, wouldn't he have possibly challenged the district otherwise and sued to keep his job?"

"Possibly. But our superintendent has a hard and fast rule on that. He basically tells our board attorney to always be ready for a lawsuit or two a year, because we are not an employment agency. When staff can't meet our ethical expectations, after we have mentored and coached them for a reasonable amount of time, then we will no longer need their services. If they decide to sue, then so be it."

"Has the district ever lost a lawsuit involving internal personnel issues?"

"Not that I recall, Linda. And the reason is that we care deeply for our employees because they are the care providers for our students. We take our time and do our best to only hire the best people. We immediately put in place a rigorous ongoing training and growth-plan process that refuses to allow an employee to not be making steady progress with his or her work. And we document. So when an employee is dismissed from this school district, it would really be a public embarrassment for that person to enter into litigation with us. We have our ducks in a row, and we are not embarrassed to proclaim that we're about kids, not about overprotecting the jobs of the adults who work for us."

"John, I feel so much better. My fear was a lawsuit. But you are saying the school district will protect this school, no matter what."

"The district will protect the students and staff in your school and the community from inappropriate behavior—period. Now what do you think you should do in regards to your out-of-control parent?"

"Well, first of all, I'm required to file the suspicion of child abuse with the social services office here in town. Second, I need to document what our other PTA officers have told me regarding the missing money and just have a discussion with all our PTA leadership to see if there is a logical explanation. Then, they can decide what action to take to recover their 'lost' money. And third, I need to meet with our dad one to one and tell him that he is hereby dismissed from his duties as a PTA officer due to his ongoing extramarital affair, which is bringing some disruption to our school climate and the school's reputation in the community."

"Sounds like a very fair plan to me. And just to make sure you've not missed a step, I'd call the board attorney and ask him to help you regarding how to do all of this by the book."

"Sounds so much more simple than what I had thought it would be now that I tell you about it, John. Really, based on the core values that I should be living by as the principal of this school, and that all of the school should be living by, I have no other options. The carelessness of this one parent must be addressed, and we must hold him accountable. And if he sues, he sues, big deal."

"You go, girl!"

"I'm not even worrying about it anymore, John. It's just what I must do."

"Linda, I am so proud of you. And yes, you will find that when you do the right things, at the right times, for the right reasons—as you are doing here in this situation—you will learn to let it go and not lose sleep over it. When you lose sleep is later when the carelessness and dysfunction in the school piles up and gets worse and worse, and you realize you allowed issues to be ignored or swept under the rug. The principals who play that game, however noble they are trying to be to keep peace, are the ones who lose sleep later on, when they realize in their heart of hearts that they let innocent people down who looked to them for strength and integrity-driven leadership."

In Leadership and Self-Deception, *the Arbinger Institute (2000) warns of the danger when any members of the organization are not able to see self the way others see them. Without personal or organizational intervention, these blind spots can lead to toxic culture issues that eventually hurt people, as well as the organization's reputation.*

SUMMARY

Linda finds out about a community leader's careless and unethical behavior, inside and outside the school, and seeks John's advice on how to address this volatile issue (this person is also one of her PTA officers and has children in the school). John recalls an earlier circumstance in his career when he had to intervene with a corrective action plan for a teacher who was an alcoholic. Linda decides to confront and address, not deny and sweep under the rug. She plans to report the behavior to the proper authorities and remove the man from his PTA duties.

16

WHEN THE FIRE GOES OUT

A mentor and a pupil growing together requires from both a thirst for learning.

John woke up with a nervous stomach. He had been dreaming about school and what it was like when the spring rolled around, when the frantic pace returned. He knew he had better pay Linda a visit.

"What do you want to talk about today, rookie?"

Linda chuckled at John and enjoyed how he had gradually built in a ritual of good-natured teasing during their visits. Only someone who had been a principal could step inside this world and have these conversations. Linda realized that, literally, John was her lifeline. She wished he could come by to chat once every two or three days.

"John, I wish I had the luxury of still being looked upon as a 'rookie.' Seems now everyone thinks I have all the answers. But I don't. And I have an interesting situation with a master teacher that I need you to help me with."

"What's the problem?"

"Well, this person is so respected in this school district and community. In fact, I had her as a teacher when I was in sixth grade and she was one of my all-time favorites."

"Is she thinking about retiring?"

"No, just the opposite. She has decided to hang on for two more years, and I'm not sure she is making a good decision."

"Does she have health issues?"

"Not anything that's all that unusual for her age. But she has 'with it' issues. What I am finding when I visit this person's room is too often unsettling. Frankly, she is just not keeping her students engaged."

"Too much lecture?"

"That's part of it. But it's just that, generally, I think she's lost touch with what this generation of kids needs to keep them focused and excited about learning day in and day out. She is not doing nearly enough computer-assisted instruction. She doesn't seem to like the concept of learning stations, and she isn't stepping back and playing the role of the facilitator for at least a portion of the day. She misses a lot of team meetings where cutting-edge instructional strategies are being discussed by her colleagues. But when I talk to her about stretching herself more, she gets tears in her eyes and asks if I think she's not doing a good job. And that's not it. I know she's trying hard and doing her best. She works as hard or harder than any teacher in our building. But I even have some parents starting to complain. They talk to other parents and feel that maybe their children aren't getting the variety of quality instruction in her classroom that other students are in our school."

"Linda, this is a dilemma that every principal has to deal with, and my heart goes out to you because it is tough. On the one hand, you have a legend who has given her life to this school. And on the other hand, you, as well as others, are observing that she is losing her edge in the classroom."

"Yes, exactly. And you are right, John, it is breaking my heart. My school council even suggested to me at our last meeting that I maybe ask her to retire. I just cannot do that. But I do have to do something, and fast."

"What does her growth plan look like?"

"It's very thorough. We've added a couple of new goals to it after some staff training in math in the fall, but I'm not sure she can pull it off. She has new teachers just out of college working around her in that hallway, and frankly, a couple of them understand differentiated learning better than anyone else in this building. They are whizzes with technology and are modeling for her something that she needs to do, but it's just so late in her career for her to make such teaching style adjustments."

"So, really, she's becoming a liability."

"Somewhat. But, on the other hand, she is a 'mother' to those young teachers fresh out of school and is such a role model. She reminds them how important it is to get to know parents well, to attend PTA meetings, to be supportive of such partnerships, and to not ever get too busy to love the kids. She's mentoring for me in ways that I, as the principal, can't do."

"Any other retirements happening this summer?"

"Not that I know of. I'd love to transfer her to a fresh and new assignment, perhaps as a reading specialist—she's so good with young kids in building those all-important reading foundations early. But I don't think there's going to be a place for her, even if she would do it."

"Well, remember, she will need to do it, whether she's comfortable with it or not, if that's where you need her the most next year. As you plan staffing details for next year, look at your talent in this building like an athletic coach looks at personnel in preparing for a season of play. Learn early on that the smartest decisions you make in helping the next school year become a better one for the kids than the current one is to play a smart chess board. What I mean by that is every staff person needs to be plugged into where he or she most benefits the school. Holding on to the same classroom, or grade, for years and years is just not the smart way to do it, although many teachers fall into that entitlement trap. Assign them where you need them most and then equip them with the training and resources so they will be successful with their new work."

"I had never thought of it that way, John. But really, it is like a ball team preparing for a new season. We all need, including me, to look at it more strategically. Does this mean I can transfer my P.E. teacher, who seems to not be interested in providing a total recreation and fitness curriculum?"

"Well, it certainly is a good time to talk to the superintendent and the other principals and see if your P.E. teacher's skills are better needed somewhere else in the district. That may be just what he needs too—a different assignment. If there is no place for him elsewhere, I suggest you explain to him what his lesson plans and actual teaching needs to look like next year and get him the necessary training this summer—even if you send him to a national conference. This is not his school. He will need to stretch and grow, just like you and every one else is doing—if he wants to have a contract in this district later on."

"You're right. There is no logic in putting this off for another year. I have been very disappointed with the lack of variety of activities in his classes and with his whole philosophy regarding physical education."

"But I don't think your master teacher who is losing her ability to stay current is in the same boat as your P.E. teacher. There are two different issues going on here. One is totally dedicated, just tired and caught in a generational gap. The other needs to make up his mind if he is truly cut out to work at this school."

"So what do I do for my master teacher who is no longer able to keep up with the pace it takes to actually do master teaching?"

"When do you get to see your budget for next year?"

"The principals are supposed to receive the first drafts next week."

"Let's think on this a bit. I'll be back in two weeks, and let's do some 'unpeeling' of your budget then. You may have some flexibility that you are not aware of."

In Leading with Soul, *Bolman and Deal (1995) remind educators that teaching is a heart thing. Without sharing of the soul, the connection that is lost between pupil and teacher is often the deciding factor as to why many, many students don't learn well in school or don't even like school.*

SUMMARY

As spring approaches, Linda notices she has a veteran and highly respected teacher who has lost some of her former skill and passion for teaching a classroom full of kids. John reminds Linda that the bottom line is building the strongest team possible for the upcoming year and getting all the staff in their individual areas of strength. He also brainstorms with her on how to keep this legend of the community as a valuable member of the instructional team. Another teacher, younger but without the commitment, needs to wake up or be removed from the school's staff plan for the coming year.

17

WHAT'S NOT WORKING? FIX IT!

I worked and worked and nothing changed, until I adjusted my strategy.

It was mid-March, and John, for the first time in many years, was thinking about some spring fishing. He had promised his dad that they'd take a retreat to the outdoors when the winter weather broke, and he was like a little kid as he packed the truck with his supplies. On his way to his parents' house, he stopped by to visit with Linda for a few minutes. As he drove over to school, he wondered why he hadn't done more getaways like this, even if during the school year, as he rushed through his career.

"I almost loved my work too much," he thought to himself. "Perhaps I would not have felt the need to retire so soon if I had been more balanced with my other passions. I did indeed practice these rules of life I am sharing with Linda, but obviously, I did burn out. So what would have made a difference? Perhaps more play, more culture, and more traveling would have made a difference. Perhaps I saved it all until now, when I should have been doing it all along."

John regained his focus as he settled into the chair across from Linda's desk. She was always so gracious and respectful to him, as she now played the role of the leader of the school, and he played the role of a visitor on her calendar for that morning. He hoped he had always made his "clients" for the day feel as comfortable and respected as she always made him feel. Many times, he remembered being way too rushed to settle into a casual conversation with whoever was there to see him—even if it was the superintendent of the school district or his wife dropping by just to say 'hi.'"

"How's that budget work going, rookie?"

"Oh my goodness, John. I never knew what efforts went into the financial part of running a school until I took this job. I have so many things I want to do next year, and so little money to really play with that is not already earmarked. I am totally at a loss for what to do next!"

"Yes, it's not as it seems when you start subtracting the returning existing staff and the various items your annual budget must pay for. Sometimes, it felt as if I'd have about $100 left over when I actually put the pencil to the paper!"

"I only wish I could say I have $100 left over! In looking at what the district is projecting for enrollment next year, it looks like I may have to reduce staff. So I'm very frustrated."

"The first peek can be depressing. Let me see what we can do."

John looked at the budget for Heritage for the coming school year and immediately noticed a couple of glitches.

"Well, I see one mistake the central office made for sure. They have your salary as being as expensive as mine had been last year, and with you being new in administration, you're not going to cost that much. So there's about $10,000 right there."

"I glanced at that, but just thought that was an automatic formula that they would adjust, but we wouldn't get to spend the difference. Hmmm, I wonder if they made that mistake on this current year too?"

"Most likely they did. No one's fault—it would certainly be easy to do. Call the district finance director next week. You probably have an extra $10,000 you can spend this year too that you didn't know you had."

"I will! Oh, this is exciting! Did you see any other miscalculations?"

"No, not at first glance. But make sure you and your budget team go over this several times before you start making any final decisions. The district office always does a great job on this, but they have many pots of money to take care of, and it's pretty routine to final things that they may have overlooked or need to adjust for a particular school based on the formulas they use."

"I will, John. Speaking of the budget team, how do I keep them focused on making unified recommendations on these money issues? I made the mistake of talking about the new annual budget at our last staff meeting, and there's been a buzz around the building ever since as everyone has a 'wish list' and a philosophy about how we should spend our money for next year."

"You didn't necessarily make a mistake. Sooner or later, about this time in the spring, the spending plan for next year does have to be brought up. It is often the most tense time of the year. We human beings can show our worst side when it comes to money issues."

"Oh, I agree. I've had staff who normally don't make a peep about anything send me e-mails about what we need, what we don't need, even what staff have done the best job this year. It's been quite disappointing."

"They will settle down. Use your budget team and work the process."

"'Work the process?'"

"Yes, there's a systematic way to do this so that everyone wins."

"I'm listening, John."

"Well, first, as you plan regular meetings with your budget team over the next few weeks, simultaneously have all of your other teams meeting as well. Go back to what you have done all year. Survey, assess, look at data, prioritize what this school needs in place so the coming school year meets even more student needs than this school year. Then revise your school's strategic plan as needed. As the end of the year nears, it will all fall into place."

"John, you make it sound so simple! Is it really that easy?"

"If you stay true to the school's core values it is. Simply have every team focused on what an authentic learning community should look like. Each team should seize this opportunity to identify what's working well, what's not, and what is needed most for next year to be the best school year Heritage has ever had in terms of what's best for kids."

"Won't they all recommend a huge list of expensive items that we can't afford?"

"Well, your budget team will need to take each team's recommendations and then synthesize the various parts into a unified whole. But you'll be surprised how similar each team's findings will be—if you will provide the tools they need to truly assess data and help them with finding the time they need to do this work right."

"But how do I help them find more time? At this stage of the year, the entire staff is swamped as we get ready for spring testing and the madness of the last weeks of the school year."

"Linda, if it were me in my first year, I'd seize the opportunity as the new principal to take a hard look at the spring's activities, and I'd cut out anything that is a tradition that no longer makes sense in terms of what's best for kids."

"You mean, like the annual circus that comes to town that we always bus the entire school to?"

"Exactly! How many years have we done that? Five in a row, I think. The kids have seen it enough to have gleaned the cultural part from it. It's a moneymaker for the community. It's not something your school has to participate in year after year."

"And all of those field trips! As a teacher, we did so many those last three weeks of the spring semester that I hated them after a while."

"Then start working on a plan now that sets policy that field trips must be spread out equally over the entire school year—not half of them packed into the last month."

"But they do indeed make the end of the year bearable for many teachers and students alike."

"That's due to the feeding frenzy culture we adults have created for the end of school. It has become a ritual not just for high school seniors but for all grade levels. And let me tell you, other professions think it's a joke, and many parents think it's a joke. I remember one dad in particular who always told me that he thought the endless playing the last few weeks of school and the hours and hours of movies during school time indicated to him that there really was not much need to even have that last month. He advised we take the month off and save the taxpayers a whole lot of money."

"But, John, was he really being fair in saying that? Don't the kids and the staff deserve a break at some point?"

"Yes, by all means. But that's what the summer vacation is for. The extra activities should be planned throughout the year, and the last month of school kept as much focused on learning as any other time of the year. But, I must admit—I put off addressing this as a principal the way that I should have because it was not worth the hassle to change the paradigm. I ended up always telling myself to work on this part of our culture later on."

"I see your point, John. We do need to make some changes in terms of the perceived misuse of time and resources. But one key barrier is that we do our annual student assessments several school days, sometimes weeks, before the end of school. Colleges wait to do finals the very last week of school, but the state requires us to do ours much earlier."

"I fully agree. And perhaps our state legislature is the body that needs to take a good look at how much time and money is being wasted as we allow our state school system to be driven by a testing contract. Might be a good letter for you to write to your state representative if you feel strongly about it. Also, content review, working on special projects that were not covered in the first eight months of the school year, transitioning kids to their next grade level, getting parents involved in some accountability over the summer if their child is behind in any subject area—all of these are simple ways to make the last few weeks of the school year more productive. Then the field trips are so much more meaningful and explainable."

"And certainly good ideas to combat the argument that kids should not even have a summer break because they forget some of what they have learned the year before."

"Exactly. Linda, I would argue, though, that if they are forgetting it that quickly, did they ever really learn it? Or are we still doing too much 'short-term memory' teaching? The routine of 'quiz on Friday, and we'll move on' is not 'long-term memory' learning. You know it, and I know it. But such an ingrained traditional approach to covering material in the classroom by a pre-set date—it's hard to change such a mind-set, and especially when it is so convenient to document that we have covered so much material in any given school year. It means absolutely nothing to many kids. It mainly works for the high achievers who independently learn on their own, whether at home on their computer or in class—too often bored long before the school day is over."

"John, you really feel strongly about this, don't you?"

"Yes, Linda, I do. When I still read in the paper that we have a nation of kids who don't know national or international history, who can't identify key U.S. cities or regions of the world on maps, who no longer rank among the globe's elite in math and science scores, and then I see the data that reveals how many American students can't read well and drop out of school? Well, let's just say I'm embarrassed that I supported a broken system of teaching and learning for all those years without doing more to change it."

"But how do you change it, John? How do we turn such a giant system around?"

"One school at a time, Linda. No, let me rephrase that: one classroom at a time."

In The Five Dysfunctions of a Team, *Lencioni (2002) addresses the reality that many, if not most, organizational teams don't really function very well—although on the surface they pretend to. He offers an alternative that works.*

SUMMARY

Linda and the budget team have been working on budgeting issues for the next school year, and she is overwhelmed by it all. John reminds her to work the process by looking at data, the school's strategic plan, priorities, and what is best for students. He assures her that when the process is trusted and utilized as it should be, the various opinions around the building will eventually zero in on wise decisions. He also urges her to take a close look at how the end of the current school year is planned, noting that something is not as it should be if the last month's schedule does not focus on learning.

18

COURAGE UNDER FIRE

I wanted to run, but knew I was needed to stay to do the right thing.

John felt bad about his tirade from the previous session with Linda. He felt like he had unloaded on her about issues there were no answers for. He was anxious to sit and offer more positive solutions this next time they chatted.

"John, come in, come in. Hope you had an awesome fishing trip with your dad. We're getting ready for spring break, and I wanted to update you on what we've jumped into!"

"Jumped into? Linda, I'm afraid to ask. Seems like the entire year you've been jumping into hot issues, and you have made huge positive changes at this school. I just wanted to apologize for how I sort of went off on a rant a little too much the last time we talked. I apo—"

Linda stopped him in midsentence. "John, I'm so appreciative of how you have helped me to look at this role from the perspective of change agent and protector of the kids. I need your pep talks more than you know. After you left last time, I went home and just wrote down the key areas that I know we are still weak in as a school. And once I saw them on paper, I had more than enough ammunition to get our school's teams focused on the monumental work we have to do now, before school is out for the summer, in getting ready for next year. And I realized I didn't have enough parents, students, and community members on those teams. So we've overhauled that weak link in our system here as well."

"Well, Linda, I must say—you sure aren't afraid to tackle the gaps as they are identified. It took me years to get us to where this school was last summer. You are way ahead of the snail's pace I moved at."

"Yes, but that comes with a price. I now have several key influencers in the building who have said enough is enough, and they basically want me out of here come summer."

"Oh, don't lose any sleep over it. I'm sure the positive mark you've made has been felt in the community and observed by the district office. Have you mentioned this to the superintendent, so he can be prepared to support you if he gets some rumblings from the ranks? He is about the same things you are about. He will not be flustered by a few resisters to change."

"No, but that's a good idea. I will make an appointment this week. I guess my main concern is that my critics are threatening to get a petition signed by several parents, who apparently will say that if I stay, their kids will be sent elsewhere to other schools next year."

"What else are you hearing they will say?"

"Just that this is not the school it used to be. That we are ruining Heritage with too many new ideas, too many changes, too much tinkering."

"Linda, I have one question: Is this school in better shape, in terms of what's best for kids, than when you found it?"

"Yes, and if we can hang in there and make these further needed adjustments by this coming fall, the sky's the limit!"

"Then that's all you need. You are an absolutely awesome school principal because every change you have implemented has been about making this school a better learning community for children. Let the detractors have their pity party, and then stay focused on getting ready for next year."

"But, John, I'm just afraid they will keep at it, keep tearing down the school's reputation, until exaggerations are circulating around, and some parents will indeed no longer have confidence in this school."

"I'll tell you what you can do. Make some time here before spring break and write a feature article for the local newspaper, simply listing all the positive things you, your staff, and the community have implemented just this year that are good for kids. Ask the paper to come and take pictures too, of the various new projects going on around the building. I'll call the editor today and ask him to take time to do this feature for your school now. And also, I've been meaning to do this: I will write a letter to the editor this week about what an unbelievable job you have been doing as my successor. Your critics may be noisy, but they do not have the 'trust' collateral I have built up in this community over the years. In other words, let me stand beside you on this one, Linda. You're taking this school to a higher level, which was my dream for Heritage when I retired."

John thought for a moment. "I will call the superintendent when I leave here this morning as well and fill him in on what I have been observing all year. Now, as soon as you can, you get out of here and enjoy your spring break!"

Tears came to Linda's eyes as she tried to say thank you to her mentor and trusted friend. "John, I never knew that on some days, it would be this hard and lonely."

"Linda, like we've discussed all year, doing the right thing, at the right time, for the right reason—which is what integrity-driven leadership is all about—is often hard and lonely. But I have found there is no greater calling than to live by such high standards. I always sleep well at night, knowing I haven't played the games with those who are weaker in character but stronger in implied influence. They have no influence when enough of the people demand that the right thing be done—in all circumstances.

John paused, and a gleam came to his eye. He then shared what his dad had told him when he was a young principal and becoming a leader in this community: "Son, you'll be tempted to sell out and practice situational ethics because of politics. You know what politics is? People lobbying for their own voices to be heard. So lobby for the important things. Lobby for those who have no voice. Lobby for a better life for this community. Lobby for the children in your school. Then you will not have become a politician. You will have become a protector of truth and hope. There is a big, big difference."

In Leading Change, *Kotter (1996) outlines how to transform organizations. And, he stresses that the rapid changes needed in being prepared for the twenty-first century will only increase. So not just a few but all organizations should beware of the need for honest self-assessment of what is still cutting edge and what practices are no longer in the best interest of those they serve.*

SUMMARY

The critics are at it again and looking for ways to make sure Linda is not the school's principal next school year. They seem to be locked in on how the school used to be, ignoring the steady improvements that have taken place in the past few months. John intervenes, writing a letter to the local newspaper praising the accomplishments of his successor, and also makes sure the superintendent knows firsthand what a difference Linda has made. He also advises her to do a "state of the school" report to be published in the local paper. He reveals to her the advice given to him by his father years earlier: to stand up for what is right and to have the courage to advocate for those who can't advocate for themselves. This, in a nutshell, is the essence of leading as a servant leader and not as a politician.

19

OVERHAUL

Sometimes, you just add some wallpaper. Sometimes, you knock a wall out and start over. It depends on if you want to live in a castle or if any shed will do.

John visited again around the first of May. Linda was waiting for him.

"I wanted to run these possible changes by you, John. Tell me if they are doable and if they will fly."

"OK, rookie. Why am I not surprised? Shoot."

"Well, the various teams have done their homework. I had them do as you suggested—we dove heavily into student data and several other factors in determining our gaps."

"And what did you find?"

"We found all kinds of things. So we're going step by step until we have a strategic plan for next school year that doesn't allow for anything to continue from this year that's not working. And we're assigning every person in this building, plus many from our community, to aggressively address the particular aspects of these gaps. It won't be easy, but we know the school must face reality. We have several fourth- and fifth-grade students still not reading well at all. Our scores in math across the board are weak. We seem to have forgotten that children need to be exposed to foreign language when they're in elementary school—when their brains absorb such new chunks of learning like a sponge."

Linda's voice raised. "And we seem to have forgotten that kids need play time and high-quality physical education. We seem to have forgotten that art and music are part of a community's culture—not just a planning time for homeroom teachers. In our madness to conform to the parts of the system that are broken, we seem to have forgotten a lot of things!"

"Linda, how did you get folks to face themselves in the mirror and finally admit that although a very good school, this place has so much more that needs to be done in truly meeting the needs of all the students here every day? What you have identified here, we talked about for years. But, quite frankly, as a collective whole, we just didn't have the energy to lay it all out there for the world to see. We made progress every year. But you have this faculty making quantum leap strides now. I am just amazed!"

"John, you forget what you told me in the very beginning. I was listening more than you thought I was. We all are following your example and living our lives by principles that we know deep down are the right way to live. We are driven by core values. We all have active, living growth plans—for professional and personal growth. We all have mentors. We are holding each other accountable. We are holding our parents and community accountable, and the district office and school board. And they all hold us accountable too."

She smiled and waved her hands with excitement. "We're having real conversations—vulnerable, authentic conversations. I can sit down with the superintendent and talk about anything, and not worry if I said the politically correct thing. You told me this was the key, and you had already preached this to your staff and modeled it. I guess when you retired and your example was missed so much here and throughout the school district, we all realized that we as individuals had to start practicing what you practiced. You had left a legacy—a philosophy that absolutely could not be allowed to fade away. It's like a snowball—it just takes off after a while and the momentum has been unbelievable."

"But what about the kids, Linda, and their parents? Are they able to handle such ongoing change and the adjustment of all phases of the school's curriculum where needed? I mean, this will indeed be a snowball, traveling downhill at high speed."

"Actually, they love it! We have decided to take your advice and make the last month of school much more meaningful. So we have dozens and dozens of parents coming in these next few days to talk about life, careers, and their educational backgrounds. Each homeroom teacher is scheduling any parent who can even come in for fifteen minutes. The response has been amazing!"

"And I'm afraid to ask . . . what about your detractors? They won't stop so easily, you know. As long as you keep implementing change, no matter how much it's needed, some will be after you."

"Who cares?! If I am leading this school by the right core values with every decision I make, then if I am disliked by some and criticized, so be it. I'm not afraid anymore—of people who are upset with me about whatever, of budget limitations, of the pressure of the job. . . . It's all just part of being a servant leader, John, and I'm okay with it. In fact, I'm enjoying this letting go and going after a future that is endless with potential for this school."

"And what is your preferable future for this school, rookie?"

"Together, as a community, I envision this school helping reshape education in this state, John. I envision all our kids reading well and doing math well by the time they leave here for middle school. I envision all these kids going on to postsecondary education, with a vast majority going on to college. I envision the community coming together to raise the funds to turn us into a national model—with state-of-the-art technology, science labs, art and music, drama, clubs, recreational programs, the best staff in the state, and the best parent involvement program too."

"Linda, you make me want to send every kid I know to this school!"

"Well you just go get them and bring them on—'cause we want them here, and we'll find the resources to meet their needs too—every one."

"But I thought you were having some problems with placing the staff you have now. How can you say you're ready for more students by fall?"

"Already fixed. We're time-sharing my P.E. teacher with another school, and using that extra half salary to assign my burned-out master teacher as a reading resource specialist for our younger grades. The district is going to pick up the rest of her salary so she can work with young teachers across the school system who need to be shown how to teach reading the right way. She's agreed to do this and is like a young woman fresh out of college, brimming with enthusiasm!"

"And your P.E. teacher? Did he buy into being assigned to two schools?"

"He had no choice. We're not about teachers claiming territory and comfort zones. In fact, the other principals are working with me to create an in-house mentoring and accountability program across the district that will identify every teacher's instructional gaps and address how to get them up to the level they need to be by summer's end. There is a whole lot of complaining going on, but the superintendent and school board are behind this 110 percent, so it's going to happen."

"But will the school board put money where its mouth is and reward these efforts with funding the addition of needed staff at each school?"

"Yes. They say that if we're willing to make this commitment, then they will stretch, too."

"Won't some teachers buck this 'moving of their cheese' so aggressively?"

"No. They really have only one option: to take professional growth as seriously as a brain surgeon—because in many ways, the two professions are very similar."

"And the other principals are cooperating?"

"Yes. All of us are embracing this commitment to higher expectations across the board as a team. We all just sat down one day and started comparing notes. It seems we all have one overriding problem: not all of our teachers are where they need to be in being able to perform their duties on the level that is required if every child in every classroom is served well during the school year. We took a random day and canvassed the school district—looking for state-of-the art, cutting-edge, research-based teaching and learning classroom cultures in motion that were inspiring to kids."

"What did you find?"

"We found too much student inactivity, too many worksheets, too many kids in rows of chairs bored out of their minds. Not an extremely high percentage, mind you, but still too many classrooms that were just sterile, dead places. We decided it was our responsibility to get rid of the deadness. So, we are."

"And you principals think you can transform the entire district in one summer?"

"We'll see how it turns out. I know this: the professional development going on this summer is customized for every person who works in this district in terms of what he or she needs the most, including custodians, cooks, bus drivers, and yes, even us principals."

"May I ask, what training will you be focusing on, Linda?"

"I'm being sent to spend a week in one of the top reading and math schools in the country, and a team from my staff is going with me. We've all attended so many 'feel good' conferences, we can't stand it anymore. It's time we go to the model schools and find out from our peers how they're making the magic happen."

In Time Traps, *Duncan (2004) addresses the curse of having too little time to do the most important things in life. Too often, principals of schools can be overwhelmed to the point of not feeling the freedom to truly make the needed changes. Thus, the madness continues: what's not working well is back next year, and what needs to be done is put on the back burner for "later on—when there's time."*

SUMMARY

After a year of mentoring and heart-to-heart conversations with John, Linda has embraced the concept of doing the right things, at the right times, for the right reasons. She and her school teams have decided on an aggressive approach to the gaps that the school still struggles with—they will be eliminated. Weaknesses in the curriculum are being corrected, and the total package of learning opportunities offered Heritage students has been expanded. Linda has approached the other principals in the district about comprehensive summer professional development for all district staff (based on what students need most), and the school board is endorsing bold, systemic change across the district—as long as the results will back up the increased support.

20

GRADUATION

A child recognized for a job well done develops a desire to go further.

The middle of May was here, and John hated to take away from Linda's time, because the end-of-the-year wrap-up was always so hectic. But she had invited him to come by and help her with some logistics.

"John, I want to do a fifth-grade graduation this year. I know Heritage has never had such a thing, but I think it's time, and a great way to celebrate the end of this school year."

"Well, I must say that I think it would be a great way to end the year strong and would add to this positive, celebratory culture you're embracing. But isn't graduation to be reserved for after completing high school?"

"I used to feel that way too, John, but this is a different time. Education as we knew it in earlier years is quickly fading away into something much less restrained by the traditional structure. Many of our exiting kids will not go all the way through school together in middle and high school. Many will move due to their parents' vocational needs. Others, for various reasons, will go to neighboring schools in surrounding districts. Some will go to private schools. Some will be home-schooled. And some—and we hope it's very, very few—will drop out and not finish high school in the traditional way. We can only hope they will eventually gain their GED—but it will not be with their friends from here at Heritage on a graduation night seven years from now."

"Good point. I guess I had just never looked into the future and faced the reality of it all, Linda. But don't you have hope that our educational system in this country is on the right track and will get better and better over these next few years?"

"Yes, I think we are getting better and will continue to meet more student needs. But, John, across the board, the reality is that only about 70 percent or less of high school freshman in the United States actually complete high school! And only about a quarter or less of those same freshman each year are going on to graduate from college! A shocking and scary indictment of our American educational system! Perhaps we have the whole formula turned upside down. Perhaps we need to take a long, hard look at how we are doing things from the very beginning—when they first enter school—and what message we send as they exit our elementary programs."

"And what message are you expecting to send with a fifth-grade graduation, Linda?"

"I'm hoping to send a message that at this stage of their academic careers, they have achieved great things. And they are now ready for the next stage—middle school. I want them feeling wonderful about what they have accomplished here at Heritage and setting high goals for these next three years in front of them."

"But doesn't all this recognition of achievement happen in elementary school anyway? Aren't we known already as the age level that seems to generate the most positive feelings toward school and that parents support the most?"

"But we're only scratching the surface, John. Perhaps we are creating an illusion for kids and parents. Perhaps we are assuming they understand that the ultimate goal is high school graduation and then on to more training and lifetime learning, wherever that may be. Perhaps we on the elementary level are also caught up in a fantasy that somehow our most at-risk kids will magically turn around when they get older. Guess what? They won't!"

"OK, OK, I see your point. But you and I both know you have fifth-graders who don't read well and who struggle in math. Do they get to be a part of this graduation of yours?"

"Yes and no. This first year, we're not excluding anybody—but we are requiring any kids who are struggling in any academic area to attend six weeks of summer school. Our school district just landed a grant for serving at-risk kids, and the superintendent has noticed all we've been doing this year to address the gaps in our school's total educational package, so he's channeled the funding our way. Heritage gets to do the pilot this summer."

"Another question: will the other elementary schools follow suit? Will the middle school adopt this philosophy as well? Perhaps they will never want to do a graduation. Won't parents from Heritage be let down if three years from now there is no similar celebration of achievement?"

"Great questions, John, and I've already talked to all the principals in our school district. They all agree: if our intense summer school program here produces results, they will join Heritage in similar exit criteria and achievement celebrations next year."

"What about the kids who don't make it?"

"The superintendent and school board are already drawing up logistics on how to route more funds into increased early intervention for all our schools. But there's a catch: Any of our existing remedial programs that aren't showing good results will be overhauled, including reassignment of personnel or reducing staff in some cases."

"So, basically, the district is saying: 'Let's do all we can on the front end—because the current model is not working. Way too many kids dropping out of school or not truly graduating with the skills and attitude to go on to postsecondary and a fulfilling, achieving life.'"

"John, I couldn't have said it better myself. Yes, as a school district, we are admitting that we can do much better. And so can our staff. And so can our students—which is why we are here in the first place as educators."

"Wow! What a shift from the traditional way of running the organization. There will be critics, you know. There will be controversy with this summer-school focus and so much accountability placed on the kids. There will be sabotage from various fronts."

"It's already happening. But because the school board is endorsing this as the best thing this district has ever done, it's going to happen. The leadership is unified, mainly because this is about kids and their futures."

"And what do the staff down on the front lines say?"

"Oh, we've had some teachers who have already jumped ship and taken jobs in other districts, or resigned and gone on to other careers, or retired. But the core is with us on this all the way. They know it's time."

"And this graduation thing here at Heritage, will you have caps and gowns—the whole ball of wax?"

"Yes, it will be a top-notch ceremony all the way, but obviously appropriate for this age group. We're not releasing the fifth-graders the last week of school and having it turned into some 'rite of passage' that inflates the students' egos into something ridiculous. But we do want it to be a very honorable, formal, festive occasion that makes every student, every family, every staff person, every community member, our district office, our school board, and our superintendent so proud of Heritage that they long to be a part of another graduation and will remember this occasion for the rest of their lives."

"And who are you going to invite to be the graduation speaker?"

"You."

In The Age of Paradox, *Handy (1994) urges organizations to practice the principle of the sigmoid curve, which states that when on the top of a wave of success, that is the time to take risks and use momentum to move on to the next wave. He cautions that to not seize such an opportunity is more dangerous, due to the fall from the wave and the lack of energy at the bottom that results.*

SUMMARY

Linda plans a celebratory, public graduation ceremony for exiting fifth-graders, wanting to send a clear message to the community about how important the total schooling process is—right on through high school and college or other postsecondary education. She also lobbies the school board for an intensive summer intervention program for her struggling students, and her fellow principals agree to adopt this program and the graduation concept the following year—if it works for Heritage. The district decides to look at all of its at-risk programs and puts the wheels in motion to overhaul any that are ineffective. Some staff across the district protest this new intensity. A few resign or move on to other districts. Most stay, knowing they are part of a revolutionary movement that will change the community forever.

21

SAYING GOOD-BYE

Our paths only crossed for a little while, but that made all the difference.

John dropped by the morning of graduation to check on the details for that evening's service and to thank Linda for being such a wonderful, coachable student all year—and to thank her for what he had learned from her.

"John, it's going to be a wonderful evening! We have the high school band coming to play, our superintendent is going to pass out diplomas as I introduce the kids one by one, and having you as our keynote speaker will be such a blessing to everyone in attendance. How fitting to have the principal who put this school on the map and whom everyone in the commu-nity just adores to celebrate with us—and share your wisdom with us."

"I'm just going to keep it short and talk from my heart, Linda. I hope that's okay."

"That will be perfect. John, I wanted to ask you, what are you going to do next year? Would you consider . . . ?"

Before Linda could finish, John answered, "I've been asked by the superintendent to coach all of his principals, using the same approach you and I used this year—just sitting down from time to time and talking leadership, and listening. Perhaps helping solve a problem every now and then, but mainly talking about core values and how to serve. So, to answer your question, yes, I will be available this coming year to coach you again. And I'm looking forward to it. I want to thank you so much for inviting me to serve in this capacity this year. I have learned so much from you. Truly, our partnership has changed my life. I feel called to provide service like this to principals, wherever needed, as long as I can keep it part-time so I can still serve in other ways at this stage too, and enjoy my family."

"Oh." Linda's eyes welled up with tears.

"What's wrong, Linda? It's fine with me if you'd rather go with another coach next year. That would not hurt my feelings at all."

"No, no, that's not it, John. You know how I'd love to keep learning from you. It's just, well, I was going to ask you to consider coming out of retirement and serving this school again as its principal."

"What? No, I've had my turn as the captain of the ship. Where are you going?"

Linda sat back in her chair and wiped her eyes with a tissue. "John, I am going to go back to the classroom."

"But, but, you can't leave Heritage so soon, Linda! This place has been . . ."

"John, my family and I have prayed and prayed about it, and I have decided I want to spend this stage of my career as a teacher right down there in the trenches with the kids."

John bowed his head for a moment. Linda thought she saw a tear in his eye. Then he smiled, stood up, and gave her a hug. "What you have meant to this school, you'll never know."

"What you, John, have meant to this school, and so many people over the years, *you* will never know. Will you make sure you mentor my successor?"

"Yes, I will be here—just as I was for you. And I will make sure what you put into motion this year will continue on."

"And I will make sure that I take your core values back to the classroom, John. I can't wait to meet my students this fall and their parents. I have an entirely different perspective on teaching now, and on relationships. Oh, to work with kids again on a daily basis now that you have helped me figure it out."

"Linda, you follow your heart and love those kids. Just embrace each day and be a blessing. Someday, you'll know when it's time to go back into the world of administration."

"The world of servant leading, John. Yes, I will indeed walk this road again—when it's time, perhaps after my own kids are grown."

John gave the speech of his life that night. He shared what he had wanted to say for years—about teaching, and learning, and passion, and family, and relationships, and serving—what experiencing all of life can really be, for anyone. And he surprised Linda with a huge video presentation of her life, set to music. Her family had rounded up the pictures for him. As her tribute concluded, the audience—everyone in attendance, even Linda's critics—gave her a five-minute standing ovation. Linda's family came up front and presented her with a dozen roses.

And her fifth-grade graduates? They surrounded her after the service for forty-five minutes of tears and hugs, and showed her a teacher's grandest hope: that she had truly made a huge, positive difference in their lives. They all, one by one, told her they would never forget her. And they didn't.

In The Servant Leader, *Blanchard and Hodges (2003) share what true leadership really is: serving others with passion and love. Such abandonment of self makes all the difference.*

SUMMARY

Linda surprises everyone by deciding to go back to the classroom until her own kids at home are grown. She has learned so much this year about what it really means to be a servant leader, she can't wait to work with a room full of children again. John agrees to continue mentoring and is asked by the superintendent to expand his coaching to all of the district's principals the following year. And he promises Linda that he will shepherd her successor, making sure what she has started will continue.

22

CLOSING THOUGHTS

> And they starved slowly, the king and queen, never knowing the peasants held the keys that unlocked the wealth of the fields, and thus, the kingdom.

In writing this book, I have tried to capture the behind-the-scenes world of school leadership. There is no more influential position in the field of education than the school principal. And there is no harder task than serving a school in such a capacity. We live in a time when how we run our schools across the land leaves much to be weighed in the balance. America is at a crossroads. Our very future seems to be on a slippery slope. We no longer play the role of the flagship global role model we formerly enjoyed, as technology has enabled the world to transform as never before. This age of endless possibility lends hope but also reveals a stark reality: America may not be prepared to remain the world's leader at the top of the chain, the shepherding nation that others have looked to for guidance for these past several decades.

Where do we turn as a nation? What do we do to guarantee we soon regain our former status? What is our hope? What is our collective vision? Much of the answer lies in how well we prepare our students of all ages for a future that is changing at warp speed. With our current state of affairs that seems to promote survival of the fittest—the rich get richer, the poor get poorer—and with high school dropout rates, illiteracy, and poverty still at embarrassing levels, with a high percentage of college students ill-prepared to complete a degree, with reading and math scores very mediocre, and science and technology losing ground to other nations, with an entire society overweight and out of shape (and with health-care plans that don't serve their patients well), and a volatile economy that has lulled us into the toxic habit of mortgaging our future for the sake of temporary luxury, America as we know it is quite possibly like the Titanic in the first few minutes after it struck an iceberg. The terminal damage was underneath the surface, but it was there nonetheless—and there was not a thing anyone could do. Have we lost our way? Have we strayed from our core values, our northern compass?

With the right comprehensive education plan in place, perhaps there is still time. With quality, age-appropriate, and challenging teaching and learning going on in every classroom, an elementary school can literally reshape a community almost immediately. Then, those kids go to middle school prepared. Later, they are ready for high school. And from there, they are equipped for college and other postsecondary training. Thus, in adult life, they are well educated and cultured, with an understanding of the core value of giving back to the community and the society they live in. They hold themselves accountable to live productive, serving, fulfilling lives that make a difference. Why? Because that's how they were taught in school—one year at a time, classroom by classroom.

It doesn't sound complicated, does it? It's not. But somewhere along the way, the ideals of our forefathers have gotten lost in this illusion that Utopia is a right, not a hard-earned privilege, that the individual's rights far exceed the common good, that it is easier to give those who won't work a check for groceries than to give them a job that allows them the dignity of earning their keep, and that it is easier to build more prisons to house the undereducated (who have turned on society because it has failed them).

And somewhere along the way we lost the fundamental principles of goodness and integrity. For the American dream to work, personal responsibility, character, and strong morals are not just an option—they are essential. Such core values were built into the framework that shaped this great nation by people of wisdom who understood how the grand experiment of democracy would go awry if unrestraint was the idol that took hold, as freedom for all would turn loose all the passions mankind could dream up.

So, to my fellow educators—whether parents, preschool, elementary, middle school, high school, adult education, college, technical school, military, or other—we all stand in the gap. As fate would have it, we carry on our shoulders the very future of our society. May we serve in this role with wisdom. May we wage the battle against ignorance and selfishness with courage. May we not let this great miracle of the human race—America—go down without a fight. May each of us one day be able to look back over our lives, as our bodies tire and wear down, with a proud look of peace and with a heart that knows we fought the good fight.

And if then this civilization as we know it has regressed into a lesser experience for those who follow, we will at least have done all we knew to do. Yet, on the other hand, what would this world look like with every human being fully educated and giving back to society? What would our country look like? What would our state? What would our region? What would our community? What would our Creator allow us to do if his people were using their talents so wisely? It is certainly a future worth dreaming about.

In The Paradox of Success, *O'Neil (1993) reminds us that, too often, winning at work means losing at life. This book is not about "winning." Instead, it is about finding a better way to lead our schools and boldly and effectively serve our children and communities.*

REFERENCES

Allen, D. B., and D. W. Allen. 2004. *Formula 2 + 2*. San Francisco: Berrett-Koehler.

Arbinger Institute. 2000. *Leadership and Self-Deception*. San Francisco: Berrett-Koehler.

Ashkenas, R., D. Ulrich, T. Jick, and S. Kerr. 2002. *The Boundaryless Organization*. San Francisco: Jossey-Bass.

Blanchard, K., and P. Hodges. 2003. *The Servant Leader*. Nashville: J. Countryman.

Bolman, L. G., and T. E. Deal. 1995. *Leading with Soul*. San Francisco: Jossey-Bass.

Buckingham, M., and D. O. Clifton. 2001. *Now, Discover Your Strengths*. New York: Free Press.

Calhoun, J., and B. Jeffrey. 2005. *Prioritize!* Sevierville, TN: Insight.

Covey, S. R. 2004. *The Eighth Habit*. New York: Free Press.

Duncan, T. 2004. *Time Traps*. Nashville: Nelson Books.

Fullan, M. 2003. *The Moral Imperative of School Leadership*. Thousand Oaks, CA: Corwin Press.

Goleman, D., R. Boyatzis, and A. McKee. 2002. *Primal Leadership*. Boston: Harvard Business School Press.

Handy, C. 1994. *The Age of Paradox*. Boston: Harvard Business School Press.

Kotter, J. P. 1996. *Leading Change*. Boston: Harvard Business School Press.

Lencioni, P. 2002. *The Five Dysfunctions of a Team*. San Francisco: Jossey-Bass.

Maxwell, J. C. 2005. *The 360 Leader*. Nashville: Nelson Business.

McIntosh, G. L., and S. D. Rima. 1997. *Overcoming the Dark Side of Leadership*. Grand Rapids, MI: Baker Books.

O'Neil, J. R. 1993. *The Paradox of Success*. New York: Penguin.

O'Toole, J. 1996. *Leading Change: The Argument for Values-Based Leadership*. New York: Ballantine Books.

Pfeffer, J. 1998. *The Human Equation*. Boston: Harvard Business School Press.

Ringland, G. 1998. *Scenario Planning*. Chichester, U.K.: John Wiley.

Senge, P. M. 1994. *The Fifth Discipline*. New York: Currency Doubleday.

Von Krogh, G., K. Ichijo, and I. Nonaka. 2000. *Enabling Knowledge Creation*. New York: Oxford University Press.

ABOUT THE AUTHOR

Rocky Wallace is the former principal of Catlettsburg Elementary in Boyd Co., Kentucky. During his tenure there, the school was named a 1996–97 Kentucky and U.S. Blue Ribbon School. He began his administrative career as principal at Fallsburg School, a pre-K–8 center in Lawrence Co., Kentucky. He later worked at the Kentucky Department of Education, providing mentoring support to first-year principals. He has also served as Director of Instructional Support at the Kentucky Educational Development Corporation in Ashland, Kentucky. Rocky received his Doctorate in Strategic Leadership from Regent University in May 2007, and currently teaches leadership classes for Morehead State University's Graduate School of Education. He has authored various articles on educational leadership and school reform.

A 1979 graduate of Berea College, Wallace is married to Denise, and the couple have two daughters (Lauren, 17, and Bethany, 14). Rocky loves to spend his spare time home with his family on their farm, and in serving his church. At this stage of his career, he is passionate about helping his students and other leaders better understand the role they play in society.

ABOUT THE AUTHOR

Made in the USA
Coppell, TX
26 August 2020

34947160R00073